CASTE, OCCUPATION AND SOCIAL TRANSFORMATION

CASTE, OCCUPATION AND SOCIAL TRANSFORMATION

A Study of Artisans of Punjab

MANJOT KAUR

KALPAZ

ISBN : 978-93-5128-172-6
Price : ₹ 790

First Published, 2016

Published by

GenNext Publication
5, Ansari Road, Darya Ganj
New Delhi-110002
Mob : 9811692060
E-mail: gennext@hotmail.com

Printed at : G. Print Process, Delhi

Cataloging in Publication Data--DK
Courtesy: D.K. Agencies (P) Ltd. <docinfo@dkagencies.com>

Manjot Kaur, author.
Caste, occupation and social transformation : a study of artisans of Punjab / Manjot Kaur.
pages cm
Revision of the author's thesis (doctoral)--Guru Nanak Dev University, 2007.
Includes bibliographical references.
ISBN 9789351281726

1. Artisans--India--Punjab--Social conditions. 2. Artisans--India--Punjab--Economic conditions. 3. Caste--India--Punjab. 4. Occupational mobility--India--Punjab. 5. Social change--India--Punjab. I. Title.

HD8689.P86M36 2015 DDC 331.7940954552 23

Contents

List of Tables

List of Figures

Acknowledgement

The processes of Industrialisation, Modernisation and now with Globalisation have initiated changes in the caste status and occupation which have led to the social mobility of lower castes/occupational groups. It is accompanied with sanskritisation especially when these mobile groups transform their caste name to upper dominant castes of their areas of residence. It is this process of the Thathiar, an artisan caste group (serving, backward caste) has now become Khatri (which is a high trading caste). This present work is an attempt to understand the process of mobility. While in the occupation, the changing nature of the traditional artisanal work of Thathiar has been examined, besides discussing the diversification and modification occurred in their work over time. The occupational mobility shows various directions of change in occupation, a large number of persons in the present generation have moved towards other jobs—such as Contractor, Shopkeeper etc., in utensil making. The younger generation does not show any interest in this work because of the hard and noisy nature of the work and the lower status it carries in the occupation hierarchy.

The book, revised version of my doctoral thesis approved by Guru Nanak Dev University, Amritsar in 2007, is a study of an artisan caste, Thathiars, traditionally associated with utensil making. In the wake of industrialisation and with the process of modernisation many new forces have been unleashed into this traditional hereditary occupation of the Thathiars. The mechanisation of the work processes and intergenerational mobility point towards the diversification as well as decay of this occupation in Punjab. The findings on the process of Sanskritisation are illuminating. The study makes an invaluable addition to the body of knowledge needed for the study of social change in changing society.

I have no words to record my heartiest indebtedness and gratitude to my worthy teacher and guide Dr Gurpreet Bal. She has been constant source of inspiration. Without her constant encouragement, generosity and valuable critical comments this study would not have reached its present form. Once again I feel eternally obliged to her.

Heartful thanks to Dr Paramjeet Singh Judge, Dr Harish Chander Sharma and Dr S.S. Narang for their cooperation and guidance.

I am grateful to the Head and worthy teachers of Sociology Department, who showed concerned in my work.

I am also delighted to acknowledge the Sociology Department, Library Staff and Sikh Reference Research Library Khalsa College, Amritsar; Punjab University, Chandigarh; Punjabi University, Patiala; Ratan Tata Library, Delhi who rendered me necessary help from time to time.

I am also grateful to the Municipal Corporation Office with their great help I could get the voter's list of the wards.

I am very much beholden to my parents, husband, daughter, close relatives and friends for enthusing me to complete this research work.

Manjot Kaur

1

Introduction

Beginning in the mid-nineteenth century, and gaining speed in the 1950s, a large modern industrial sector has grown up in India. The country now meets many of its own industrial needs and exports such diverse products as gemstones, trucks and cars, iron and steel and clothes (McLeod, 2004). The word 'industrial revolution' usually refer to that complex of technological innovations which, by substituting machines for human skill and inanimate power for human and animal force, brings about a shift from handicraft to manufacture and, so doing, gives birth to a modern economy. The industrial revolution has already transformed a number of countries, though in unequal degree; other societies are in the throes of change; the turn of still others is yet to come. The industrial revolution began in England in the eighteenth century, spread from there in unequal fashion to European countries and a few areas overseas. The heart of the industrial revolution was an interrelated succession of technological changes. The material advances took place in three areas: (1) substitution of mechanical devices for human skills; (2) inanimate power particularly steam in place of human and animal strength; (3) marked improvement in the getting and working of raw material, especially in what are now known as metallurgical and chemical industries (Landes, 2003).

Concomitant with these changes in equipment and process went new forms of industrial organisation. The size of the productive unit grew: machines and power both required and made possible the concentration of manufacture and shop and home workplace gave way to mill and factory (Landes, 2003).

It is argued that successful industrialisation is possible only if certain institutional and organisational conditions are met (Moore, 1968; Hughes, 1958). Among these, important are: mobile and skilled labour force, access to technology, monetary basis of exchange, markets for the products, and sources of investment fund. The institutional framework and the structure of relations required for an industrialised society are believed to be markedly different from those associated with hunting or agricultural economies (c.f. Dak, *et.al*. 1987).

In this study an attempt has been made to analyse an artisan group, the Thathiars which have undergone tremendous transformation in the nature of their work due to industrialisation. The discussion in this introductory chapter is divided into six sections: (1) The effect of industrialisation on handicrafts, (2) The role of artisans, (3) The artisans of Europe, (4) The artisans of India, (5) Transformation in Thathiars and (6) Methodology used in the light of the objectives.

1. Effects of Industrialisation on Handicrafts

A fascinating shift in the nature of industrialisation as also definitions and attitudes concerning the production of goods is taking place as we go into the 15th year of the globalisation process. In the area of handmade goods, both crafts and textiles, even as countries like India are learning to convert their weaknesses into strengths. In China, mechanisation is efficiently organising itself to imitate the handwork of India to encroach upon the market for India's special skills. It is obvious that such competition comes into play because the demand is palpably there. In the post-industrialised world, with its multinational production and marketing systems, branded goods and the similarity of products wherever they may be sold, the very non-standardised and multicultural nature of handicrafts provides the competition and welcome contrast.

Obviously the handicrafts sector consisting of the producers, wholesalers, retailers, technicians including designers, and most importantly, the policy-makers, must begin to look at itself as an industry of the non-industrialised, and prepare to gear itself up for the enormous challenge that lies ahead. Industry is merely the organised production of goods arising out of the combined and systematised work of man with machine. Industrialisation has conventionally meant the dominance of machine over man and of capital over labour. Crafts in contrast can be termed an industry where the machine does not dominate and its much decentralised structure prevents the exploitation by a capitalist tycoon sitting far away, controlling production and workforce. We need no longer be bound by the old attitudes towards what is accurately but slightly condescendingly termed as 'cottage' or 'village' industry. We have become stultified in an image of industry representing standardised, monotonous, centralised production. If these are the images of the industrial age, we can now alter ourselves for the post-industrial age of information technology and globalised production of mass-produced goods.

Crafts, by their very nature, are not mass produced. But if people are working with their hands, albeit with the assistance of tools and machines, producing goods required in a wide market space, selling to make profits and thereby contributing to national wealth, crafts can be termed as a decentralised creative industry where the human mind and hand is more important than the small machines and tools they use. Here the machine is the instrument of the maker, owned by the maker or by the community, therefore, a world of industry without industrialisation in the traditional sense, and there is both ample scope and need for this to come out of and to that extent craft is free from domination and exploitation. There is disorganised, diminishing and low-end pro le that it has been carrying for long. India is a country with over a crore of handloom weavers and an equal, if not larger, number of craftsmen engaged in diverse crafts from pottery to basket making, stoneware, glassware, handmade paper products and multifarious other utility items made out of locally, available materials. This is because of negative compulsions in that these artisans know no other skill due to centuries of immobility arising out of rigid caste structures, and because of a lack of viable economic options (www.culturaleconomics.atfree).

2. The Role of Artisans

Artisan is a self-account worker or a wage earner engaged in the production of certain items. He acquires the skills traditionally or through informal training (Mishra and Rao, 2004). It is the nature of the artisan to express himself through the invention, creation, manufacture, repair, and manipulation of things. These can be artistic masterpieces, technological crafts, or mechanical devices. In prehistoric times, artisans were involved in such ancient arts as pottery-moulding, basket-making, weapons, tool-making, cave-painting, and hut-building. In historical times, an artisan has typically made his livelihood in such occupations as blacksmith, craftsman, and tradesman — a member of a guild who passed his skills on to apprentices. There were numerous other cottage industries, and there was always need for a scribe when not everyone was literate. Whenever and wherever there is something that needs to be made, there is an artisan — ready, willing, and able to make it. And whatever occupation an artisan nds himself in, he will always apply a high degree of skill and expertise to it. Artisans are technicians in whatever they do (Michael Teaching–The Artisan Role.htm). Day-to-day living is often a bore for the artisan, who delights in being a connoisseur of anything novel in life, leaving the monotonous grind of the nine-five workplace to other roles that crave the responsibility and inherent demands of such an existence. Often so fiercely innovative and ahead of their time that they find themselves in stark contrast with the rest of society, artisans feel out of touch with the world, and simply drop out of circulation. Even for artisans who contribute and adhere to more productive lifestyles, there's often a random sense of order in the way they focus on projects, and usually their world is littered with a confusing array of unfinished projects, sometimes literally strewn everywhere. Of course, where the artisan might see this type of system as being completely logical and ordered other roles might be completely baffled by this seemingly disorderly approach to life. Artisans are concerned with all forms of structure, and are most likely to complete their life tasks through expressing some sort of structure, whether actual or theoretical. Artisans tend to want to create structure in their lives, and to expect others to adapt to it. Artisans are acknowledged by access to projects and iconic awards. Artisans have many channels of input. The sense associated with artisans is balance. Artisans often have to come to realise that not everything can be reduced to structure (message from michael.com).

During the census operations between 1881 and 1931 in the Punjab, as in other parts of India, a large number of artisan castes expressed their desire for upward mobility by returning themselves as belonging to 'upper' caste. The census operations were taken as an instrument to gain upward social mobility by the artisan caste by returning themselves as belonging to higher caste. In the Punjab, tendency to return as belonging to 'upper' caste among the artisan and other castes was first noticed in 1881. Some persons of 'lower' castes had returned themselves as Sheikhs, Pathans, Mughals, etc. (Sharma, 1979). Expansion in trade and commerce also meant an increase in guilds and the employment of many more artisans. The term guild is usually taken to mean an organisation of the workers in a special craft (Weber, 1950), thus in the middle ages there were guilds of carpenters, weavers, goldsmiths, iron-mongers etc. The guild had two principal aims which contrast sharply with the aims of our own industrial system. First, the guild tried to preserve equality, at least among the masters of the craft. The second aim of the guild system was to maintain its economic position in society (c.f. Schneider, 1969). The artisan's guild was, in fact, the local caste guild of manufacturers of particular commodities, the head of the caste ensuring the maintenance of traditional methods and standards. The guild provided education as well, though not 'formal' education, which remained in the hands of the Brahmins and monks. The guilds, by restricting membership to artisan of a particular craft, were centres for technical education (Thapar, 1968).

The age-old specialisation of artisans in certain occupations has been challenged by industries. The role of artisan has been taken over by the machines which produce in bulk and that too in a very little time. In a way, rural artisans have become victims of urban industry. It is, therefore, quiet relevant to examine the position of artisan production which is in transformation. The main reason for shifting the occupation is the decrease in the demand for the craft products. Earlier, the artisans were in great demand for their monopoly over certain skills, but now the growth of industries has come up as a strong competitor against them. Change has not taken place at one point of time; rather it occurred gradually (Bal, 1995).

3. The Artisans of Europe

A recent study by James (2000) has been published on the artisans in Europe's cities and towns from the late middle ages into the era of industrialisation. Artisans were skilled people who fashioned artefacts with their hands and tools but without the aid of machinery. Until recently, histories of artisans described craftsmen as pre-industrial skilled workers destined to be crushed by the juggernaut of mechanised, factory production.

The guild was a central cog in a theoretical system of order that emerged in the late middle ages which historians have come to call corporatism. Probably the best known privilege that guilds possessed was the monopoly over the manufacture and sale of particular items. To be sure, guild statues or by-laws everywhere did specify such a privilege and specific provisions were made for preventing one guild's craftsmen from encroaching upon another's, a very pressing concern among tradesmen working with the same materials like leather, wood and metal. Guild by-laws also regulate economic relations within the guild. No master, for instance, was permitted to monopolise the purchase of raw materials or the hiring of workers.

The map of the late medieval and early modern (1300-1914) European economy as the economic historian Vries (1994) observes, can best be thought of as a collection of regions with cities and towns as their focal points. From the high middle ages onwards, a process of increasing economic integration occurred first within and later between these regions. The process was uneven, but Europe's cities gradually were stitched together in an increasingly tight commercial system that more and more brought the countryside into its orbit. Within their increasingly obsolete walls, cities constituted the infrastructure of the economy, the site where a great deal of craft production was organised, goods distributed, and capital attracted and invested. Of course, such a process of network creation and integration was far from linear, happening more rapidly in some areas than in others.

What happened during the late eighteenth and nineteenth centuries which fundamentally transformed the artisanary of Europe's cities was the convergence of multiple forces — legal, political, intellectual, demographic and economic—during the era of industrialisation and one result was the destruction of the culture of the artisan and the transformation of his and her identity. Of course, it did not happen overnight (it took 150 years). During the eighteenth century especially in England, we find the language of the law shifting from a defence of traditional collective rights to one of utility based on individual rights. Artisans had "since time immemorial" based their sense of status upon widely held notions of customary legitimacy. As the law shifted ground, however, the artisan's claim of traditional, collective right lost its bite. As a result, craftsmen were confronted with a new legal world, and had to adapt to it. In France during the revolution, the law changed more abruptly and artisans promptly responded to it. A declaration by the National Assembly on August 11, 1789, simply called for the 'reformation of the trades', but guilds were only officially abolished by the Allarde law enacted on March 17, 1791 (Pontet, 1997).

Much current research points toward the last quarter of the nineteenth century in some parts of Europe, the early twentieth century in other parts (southern Europe) when we see a quantum transformation in production, processing and retailing. This transformation was enabled by regularisation of demand smoothed by the dramatic changes in transport and communication, price elasticity, capital intensive and increasingly standardised production culminating in the assembly line, and, ultimately, the scientific management principles of 'Taylorism' and 'Fordism'. Amid such changes, artisans did not suddenly disappear, but they did become something altogether different, gradually but ineluctably more integrated into production and distribution networks that were controlled by large capital. Intensive sub-divisions of tasks and sub-contracting continued apace and as independence became increasingly a chimera (horrible creature of the imagination), artisans gradually evolved into mechanics, shopkeepers or wage workers. In Germany, where industrialisation after 1870 was rooted in large-scale finance and centred on capital goods production, small commodity workshop production declined noticeably. In 1882, 60 per cent of German industrial manufacturing enterprises still had five or fewer employees, but by 1907 only 31 per cent did. In France in 1906, 10 per cent of the workforce was employed in large factories of more than 500 employees. What these figures suggest, and current research continues to affirm, is the existence from mid-century of a dual economic structure which had an artisanal and an industrial face, but one that saw the balances tilting decidedly away from artisanal favour (James, 2000).

There was no legal restoration of corporatism in the nineteenth century, of course, and its gradual if relentless displacement by liberal capitalistic market culture and in many places, an intrusive state apparatus, ultimately recast the mould within which artisans fashioned their identity. Corporate attitudes among craftsmen did not disappear at the same pace everywhere; they were largely gone from England by 1850, from France probably by 1890, while they lingered longer in Germany. In any case, by the turn of the twentieth century one would be hard pressed to find an artisan who self-consciously defined himself in terms that his forebears of a century or two earlier had. Instead, he was now a skilled worker, a mechanic, a shopkeeper and he thought of himself as such. The nineteenth century also brought a crystallisation of the processes that separated the artisanary into productive and retail segments that historians have traced to the eighteenth century in some trades but to the nineteenth in many more, and this no doubt is central to the story of the transformation of the artisan (James, 2000).

Therefore, the impact of industrial development varies from one country to another, one artisan group to another according to the relevance and demand of the group for the modern work.

A recent study by Hanna (2011), deals with the artisans and guilds of the Ottoman Empire. Scholars have written about artisans in Istanbul, Bursa, Aleppo, and Jerusalem. More speci□cally, this study work on with the artisans in Cairo follows the same tradition as the work of two other scholars, namely Andre Raymond, whose work was fundamental in showing the socio-economic status of artisans and their changing relations to the Mamluk class, and Pascale Ghazaleh.

One of the issues the study tackles is how to study artisans and guilds, not only in the context of a traditional society and economy, but rather in the context of a period which was undergoing signi□cant changes (1600-1800), due to both local and to regional conditions.

The approach it uses is that of "history from below," since one of the questions that it addresses is how to de□ne a role for these artisans and guilds in the context of the prevailing commercial conditions of the period, but also as a source of developments in the nineteenth century. The study also addresses the core-periphery model of the world systems approach and attempts to include artisans in this model. In other words, rather than discuss the core-periphery model solely in relation to merchants and commercial activity, it incorporates artisans and their products into the model.

Thus, on the one hand it deals, at a micro level, with the individual lives of artisans, following the lives of a few artisan families over several generations, focusing on their work and on their relations to guilds and the economy, as well as to their families and colleagues. At the macro level, these artisans are placed in the context of the broad global and regional changes of the period 1600-1800, namely the greater world trade and more intensive commercial exchanges taking place worldwide. By combining these two different levels, links could be made between the local and the global, between the artisans who worked their product and the expanding horizons of international trade (Hanna, 2011).

The question around which the study revolves is how these artisans fared in the light of these conditions. The study comes up with the idea of "trade without periphery," a term to describe the period as one during which the region as a whole underwent a certain level of commercialisation, but did not undergo the peripheralisation of its economy, as happened in the nineteenth century. The same concept could be applied to other regions, such as other parts of the Ottoman Empire or India, which experienced similar conditions, and where commercialisation brought about a certain social mobility, both upwards and downwards.

4. The Artisans of India

The review of literature reveals that a few studies have been conducted on various artisan groups in India. These studies have been conducted on the Blacksmiths, Traditional Potters, and the Chamars and, on the artisans in general.

Chicherov (1971) has shown that the surviving artisans are now becoming commodity producers. This process proceeded in two directions. Firstly, the artisan have expanded and strengthened their ties with both the market outside and the village community. Secondly, the village community has started maintaining its artisans. But, at the same time, the commodity relations between the peasants and the artisans are being replaced by cash nexus.

Shukla and Anima (1981) have shown the continuity as well as change in the occupation of artisans. They have found change in many cases, but no caste group which traditionally performed important functions in the village economy has completely ceased to do so. Most of the members of Ahir, Teli, Nai, Dhobi and Chamar castes are still carrying on their activities.

Bose's (1982) study has focused on various features of production organisation and market relations of Potters of Gujarat. He has shown the persistence of the traditional system. Industrialisation has not occurred at an equal rate and extent in all regions and the same is its impact on different artisan groups. The production is still based on family and kin, where recruitment of outside labour is almost negligible and most of them work on *jajmani* relations. All those Potters, who have changed the relations and have come to market situation, generally develop two kinds of relations:h (i) the Potter receives a contract from a contractor to supply the necessary number of pots to him; in turn the contractor sells them in the market; and (ii) the potter himself goes to the market and sells wares, besides, selling them to villagers (c.f. Judge and Bal, 2006).

Sharma's study (1986) proposed that the process of industrialisation in the area of leather work would become an instrument of socio-economic development and consequently of social mobility for the artisans belonging to the Chamar castes. The Chamar caste members were engaged in the tanning and shoe-making. This study was conducted at Karnal where many small scale units carrying out shoe production with the involvement of traditionally skilled leather workers from the Chamar castes and from here shoes were marketed to other parts of India. The migrants to Karnal have come from places as far as Agra, Aligarh, Bulandshahar (UP) and Ludhiana.

The Jalandhar sports industry is the one case from Punjab, which has shown tremendous socio-economic development of the low-caste artisans. The industrial development especially with reference to Chamar artisans has certainly made considerable difference in economic terms. The leather workers working in the shoe industry in the contemporary times are relatively better off than their elder generations. This also indicates intergenerational upward economic mobility.

Though, shoe-making is carried out by the Chamar caste, yet trading in shoes and other leather items no longer remain in their domain. It is now increasingly taken over by other business communities, such as Banias, Khatris and even Brahmins. In fact, men of high castes have monopolised the leather business as owners and employers to a great extent as it. This is a very paying business in pecuniary terms. Shoe-making has also acquired the status of an organised occupation having its own market at local, regional, national and international level. This has helped in the survival of traditional skills and has created demand for these skills in the market situation. The changes occurring in the position of the occupation as such have become a major motivating factor for the Chamar artisans to adopt shoe-making as their career.

Another artisan group, i.e., the Potters have been studied by Krishnan (1989) working in Delhi. As they are producers, the market is central factor in their life and work. While most of the Potters are from the rural areas, there is noticeable trend of urban migration on their part. In view of expanding and changing contours of the market, specific objective of the study is the growth and widespread dispersal of industries and to increase the level of earning of artisans. The study identifies 40 localities of the potters in Delhi. Murtikar, a distinct section, who makes clay toys and icons live in 14 localities. The total population of Kumhars in the 40 localities is 9,063. The total number of Kumhar households in the identified localities is 1,899. The Potter population has come to consist of a large number of migrants from rural areas of Rajasthan, Haryana and Uttar Pradesh and also of a sizeable number whose roots have always been in Delhi city. The process of migrations is still going on.

The Potters of Delhi manufacture both traditional and new products side by side. These bear the distinct impress of the urban and metropolitan pattern of life and resultant needs and demands. In the case of the pottery goods, the consumer profile is different. Its market largely consists of lower income groups. Pottery goods tend to be largely disposed of at a large number of local points and there are very little movements to central points. More than 70 per cent of Kumhars have given up pottery in this generation and joined other occupations on account of market shrinkage for their products.

A study has been conducted by Bal (1995) on the Blacksmiths as an occupational group from the perspective of continuity and changes both in rural and urban context in Punjab. The smith was traditionally a nail-maker and fixed horse shoes. He made axes, chisels, hammers, saws etc. In Punjab, smiths engaged in making and repairing the agricultural implements and other household and construction articles. They generally hail from one endogamous group viz. Lohar. Besides, the Lohars, there are three other endogamous groups-Ramgarhias, Sikligars and Gaduliya Lohars who are traditional smiths in this region. In this study, three categories representing three levels of technology–low, medium and the modern—were used to examine the activities of Blacksmiths. To represent the first category, traditional smiths were taken from twenty different villages. In the second category the smiths engaged in the registered steel re-rolling units of Punjab were examined. In order to study the third category, the smiths of registered industrial manufacturing units were examined.

The powerful forces of industrialisation have weakened the bond of caste with occupation. People have crossed the caste barriers and have taken up other occupations. This study shows 19 different caste groups have taken up smithy as their occupation. This includes both the traditional smiths and non-traditional caste groups. The other caste groups are Brahmin, Jat, Khatri, Bania and Rajput besides other backward and scheduled castes.

Smithy as an occupation has undergone tremendous transformation, as a result of the impact of industrialisation. Particularly with regard to change in techniques, mode of work, diversification of work, increase in profits, organisational structure, place of work and joining of non-traditional castes. The experience of changes varies with the level of smithy such as a few of the traditional smiths have introduced changes. Smiths engaged in medium and modern industries have pointed out that machines are revolutionary improvement over the conventional and obsolete tools as they have raised the output and have drawn a wider market leading to more profits.

Sharma's study (1996) on, "Artisans of Punjab" reveals that due to rapidly changing socio-economic environment in the British Punjab, the framework of traditional relationship between the artisans and land-owners was significantly altered. A considerable proportion of the artisans moved out of the village, and in many cases, altogether changed their occupation. These circumstances had a bearing on their demographic distribution as well.

The artisans were slow to respond to the combined effect of the various developments like colonisation, extension of cultivation, commercialisation of agriculture, development of industry, the means of communication and spread of literacy. The process of change was gradual and complex. Change of occupations by the artisans in the early stages was, thus, largely towards agriculture and later on towards industry where they could employ their skills and energies more effectively and advantageously. These changes, however, did not appreciably help them to improve their social evaluation. They continued to be evaluated with reference to their caste, which remained the source of frustration and discontent. The increasing educational opportunities provided another avenue for change to the disoriented and discontented artisans.

Parthasarathy, (1999) deals with some aspects of artisan production as it is carried out in rural areas in Gujarat. A majority of the artisan households referred to in the study reported that there has not been any change in the type of products made during the previous decade, though a significant proportion of the households of Potters, Chamars and Carpenters reported discontinuation of the production of some of the goods produced by them previously. In contrast, a very small proportion of households of potters and shoe-makers reported diversification into new item during the same period. It was observed that over two-fifths of artisan households produce items against prior orders. As regards mode of payment, over 75 per cent of the households reported payment in cash as the prevailing method. A majority of the households that derive their income from artisan occupations had no access to land. Since the artisan occupations require skills that are traditionally inherited, the levels of education among artisan households were also explored. Most of the workers had their skills developed through informal or on-the-job training, a fact that indicated the persistence of the hereditary system of skill transfer. Very few artisan groups reported having received specific training related to their present vocation. Overall, the rural artisans face difficult market conditions. Other opportunities apparently lay in non-traditional production related activities like machine fitting that require technical skills. A key issue is to identify policy measures and institutional structures which will facilitate the transition from traditional to non-traditional skill-intensive activities in rural areas.

Douglas' study (2006) on the Weavers artisan-capitalist and the transformation of the informal economy (1940-1960) indicates that they were able to expand the realm of their economic activities in great part because of the new power they had acquired in the artisanal towns of western India. State actors depended upon them to win elections and to generate support for projects of economic development.

The informal economy in short depended upon the emergence of a particular political order. The explosive growth of the 'decentralised' sector in textiles after the period covered here was possible because this order was already in place by the early 1960s. Increasingly, new forms of merchant capital poured into textile production in places like Surat and Bhiwandi, confident that their investments would not be undercut by substantial union activity or by massive state regulation. Key to this development, of course, was keeping the scale of industry small, since in larger industries a host of rules still did apply. The informal economy thus reproduced itself and expanded, often at the expense of other kinds of economic forms like the mills.

5. Transformation in Thathiars

The brass and copper ware industry was one such industry which was never very widely spread in rural India. It had always been primarily an urban industry, but since the beginning of the industrial period, it had begun to concentrate in big towns to an even greater degree than before. The different forms of organisation found in this industry were the independent artisan, the master worker with one or two assistants, and the workshop. The former two were predominant in the smaller towns. The industry was a flourishing one and the demand for its products was very large. Differentiation and specialisation of operations were proceeding at a rapid speed and machinery was being slowly introduced. All this resulted in a movement towards the concentration of the industry in a few big towns, and the workshop was becoming the typical form of organisation. In many of the larger towns workshops employing as many as twenty or more persons were to be found. In the brass and copper ware industry, on the other hand, the processes were very varied and the work was split into a number of different operations, for each of which a specialised workman could profitably be introduced. The introduction of small machinery for certain simple operations was also possible (Gadgil, 1972).

Sahay (1967) also reveals in a study that the castes once devoted to their specific traditional professions are taking to new occupations as in the case of the Brahmin, Rajput, Lohar, Kumhar, Dhobi and Chamar castes. This has happened because their traditional profession has ceased to be profitable while other jobs give them a better opportunity to earn and fulfill their needs within the growing monetary economy.

A study on "The Artisans of Benaras" by Kumar (1988) indicates that the brass and copper industry forms a contrast with the silk industry in that it has been in increasingly troubled straits for the past seventy to eighty years. It has three distinct branches: the manufacture of domestic utensils, of idols and other Puja (worship) articles, and of decorative pieces. Metal workers today, in contrast to weavers, have a clear sense of loss. All those who manufacture Puja articles or do reposse work, face little problem of demand, and rarely complain of prices. Of those working at utensils of one kind or another, approximately 50 per cent have left the occupation in the last thirty to fifty years judging by information from individual families. As the Royal Commission on Labour noted in 1931, artisans worked very long hours, but this did not signify a busy market. The metal utensils industry was "steadily going down and the men whose ancestors had been engaged in it for generations had to work harder and harder to eke out subsistence." The process of shifting from metal working continues to the present day. In some parts of Benaras, the industry has died out within living memory.

According to Bhandani's study (1999) the size of urban craft production in Marwar may be judged by a study of the evidence about the urban population and its composition. Marwar had in the time of Nainsi about 25 towns and the urban population was about 17 per cent of the whole population. Nainsi provides information relating to various professional craftsmen, labourers and other city dwellers.

This study shows the records of the houses of different castes of brass workers, Kasera-Thathera (brass and copper smiths), Bharwara (brass and copper smith) and Kharadi jaradi (brass polishers) included the houses of all these castes under one leading brass/copper workers for comparison with modern figures. The workers involved in brass work are recorded in four towns out of eight in the year of 1660. In 1891, recorded in these four towns, the population of brass workers appears to have declined considerably. From the above comparison, we can say with certainty that brass and copper ware industry was comparatively better developed in 1660 than in 1891, at least in respect of the size of urban employment that it provided.

With the advent of technological advancement and industrialisation, traditional artisans who were perfect in their work, most of them have joined as skilled workers. So many other alternations and differentiations can be seen in this process. The work has been divided among manufacturers, contractors, wholesalers and retailers. Industry had a great impact on the artisanal work. Some works have got wider demand than they earlier had. With industrial growth, functional specialisation and interdependence among different parts of society, there have grown up numerous and powerful occupational groups and at the same time some of the occupational groups are in the process of decay. Still, some other occupational groups are experiencing transformation due to industrial and agricultural development (Bal, 1995).

The process of change during the British period though slow had set the course of social change among the Thathiars. It may be partly due to slow growth of industry and the limitations of the artisans to effectively respond to new opportunities created by industries. In the process of modernisation and industrialisation, they are destined to lose some of the skills, while some others are further being utilised in the industries. Since change varies with the degree of industrialisation, we can find various levels of transformation, which have taken place among utensil-makers or Thathiars.

6. Methods of the Study

The main objective of the study is to explore the changing nature of the relationship between caste and occupation. It is to examine the changes which have been taking place in an artisan caste group and also the process and pattern of change in its occupation. The following are the broad objectives of the study:

7. Objectives of the Study

1. To know the social, economic, cultural and demographic aspects of the Thathiars.
2. To identify the changes as these are taking place in the caste system i.e., in its features, practices and processes of change among the Thathiars.
3. To examine the emergence of class within the caste, that is the emergence of economic inequalities within the caste group in two contexts–
   (a) Representation in the social, political and religious sphere.
   (b) Patterns of interpersonal and inter-caste relations.
4. To explore the changes which are taking place in the occupation in context of–
   (a) Skill formation, work organisation and techniques of work.
   (b) The transformation in the production process.
   (c) The economic and political organisation of the Thathiars. Particularly for procuring the raw material, marketing of the goods and resolving the issues of conflict.

5. To find out their process and pattern of occupational mobility and status enhancement.

8. Selection of the Respondents

Jandiala Guru, a town famous for utensil making was chosen for study. It is a town with municipal committee. As per the Census 2001, the total population of the town is 23,689

Founder of Jandiala guru (Guru Baba Hundal Ji)

*Source:*www.tribuneindia.com/2005/20015006/a plus.htm#2

as against 19,283 in Census 1991. Out of this population, males are 12,598 and females are 11,091. Its area is 14.5 square kilometers. It is situated on the G.T. Road and also connected by road with Goindwal and Tarn Taran. The town was named as Jandiala after Jand, the son of its founder. The town had a mud boundary wall with seven gates. In 1767, Charat Singh, grandfather of Maharaja Ranjit Singh invaded the town to teach a lesson to the Niranjania Guru, who had submitted and accepted services with Ahmed Shah Abdali. The town is predominantly inhabited by Jains. There are three Jain temples in this town. Presently, Ratnagar Suri is the head of this community. Majority of the Jains are engaged in the work of utensil selling, because this work has flourishing market in Jandiala Guru.

Town is also famous for religious and devoted to god people and thus this city has many gurdwaras and mandirs. There is a gurdwara 'Baba Hundal ji Tap Asthan' built in the memory of Baba Hundal. Akhand Path (non-stop recitation) of Sri Guru Granth Sahib is a special feature of this gurdwara. Another gurdwara built at the place where Baba Hundal was born.

This historical place has good proportion of metal workers or the Thathiars. This work also provides identification to the town. It has become famous for manufacturing the different kinds of metal utensils especially in brass, copper and zinc. Most important commodities, which are exported or manufactured, are brass-vessels, metal utensils, grinders, cotton labels and oil.

The entire residential area of the town is divided into 13 wards. Out of which six wards have a majority of working Thathiars. In the wards number 2, 4 and 5, people belonging to schedule castes are residing. While wards number 9 and 11 have Jain mohallas. The ward number 6 has predominantly the Jat families and ward number 3 consists of market of the municipal committee.

Sample Size of Working Thathiars According to Wards

Sr. No.	*Ward No.*	*Working Thathiars*	*Proportion*
	12	220	110
	13	146	73
	7	92	46
	8	64	32
	1	52	26
	10	49	24
Total		**623**	**311**

Sample size of working Thathiars was prepared with the help of information collected from the office of the municipal committee and through exploratory survey of the town. The six wards i.e., number 12, 13, 10, 8, 7 and 1 have been found having high concentration of working Thathiars. A list of working Thathiars from each ward was prepared. The total number of working Thathiars in these wards is 623. In order to draw the sample the number of working Thathiars in the list of six wards was arranged in descending order. By maintaining the serial continuity of the list, every alternate case is included in the sample. Out of 311 proportions, 300 respondents were interviewed. According to every alternate case, eleven respondents were those, who kept as optional case, as among from the 300 respondents if some respondents refused to give the answer, some were unable to give the answer due to age factor or illness, unavailability of the respondents.

9. Data Collection

The data for the present study has been collected both through the primary and secondary sources. The primary sources consist of interview schedule designed for the purpose of ascertaining information on different aspects of the research problem. Secondary sources consist of information from the office of Municipal Committee of Jandiala Guru and from various census reports, books and journals. We first made a preliminary visit to the Thathiar localities and to their work places, then prepared a schedule for pre-testing.

Five respondents were interviewed, certain questions were dropped and some more were added to it. After pre-testing, the final interview schedule was prepared. Data were collected through interviews. In order to keep uniformity of the data collection, all the interviews were conducted personally with the selected respondents. In addition, method of observation was also used on various aspects of their life including their living style, place of work, working condition, how do they work, the condition of their children and their domestic activities. The interviews were conducted during rest intervals or lunch break and after working hours i.e., in the evening at their homes or shops.

To facilitate the responses, each question was read out slowly, patiently in Punjabi language to obtain correct information. Each interview took more than an hour. Sometimes, in some cases while conducting interview, it took the shape of group interview. In this situation, it was quiet tough to get proper responses of the interviewee, because everyone would be participating (number of persons was six to eight). In this condition, I would continue discussion with all of them. But, I stopped to interview that person or respondent. Again that respondent was interviewed after some time or the next day. The majority of the respondents with exceptions showed a keen interest in being interviewed. In all 300 respondents were interviewed.

10. Analysis of Data

The data collected was analysed to understand the changes that have been experienced over the years. Data analysis involved various stages like preparation of code design, code sheets and tabulation. After collecting the data, all the schedules were edited to check the completeness. All the information was compressed into meaningful and manageable categories and the categories were assigned codes systematically. Thus a clear and comprehensive code design was prepared after going through responses. All the interview schedules were coded according to the code numbers assigned to different responses. These were then transferred to the coding cards.

On transferring all the data on the code sheets, single variable and double variable tables were prepared. Percentages were calculated for the entire tables. The findings of the study have been presented in seven chapters of the thesis.

2

The Thathiars

Man's innovative talent and his urge to create beauty found expression through a variety of media such as clay, stone and metal etc. But the most potent medium that revolutionised the economic and the social structures in different periods of history is metal. The discovery of metal, therefore, be considered as one of the most remarkable and revolutionary gain of humanity (Dahiya, 1986). Thus, metal workers have an important place. They made utensils, weapons, tools, ornaments, toys and figurines etc. Metal vessels are used in India for domestic purposes. These vessels may be classed as sacrificial utensils, cooking utensils–plates, cups and drinking vessels and miscellaneous articles.

This chapter focuses on the Thathiars, an artisan caste group whose traditional occupation is utensil making. The chapter is divided into four sections. The first section deals with artisans in general. The second section is about the origin of the Thathiars and the myths on the origin of the term. In the third section, the Thathiars of other regions, besides their social customs, religion and occupations have been discussed. In the fourth section, Thathiars of Jandiala Guru form the focus of analysis.

The Artisan Castes

The term artisan is generally used in the sense of one who possessed practical skill in a particular trade or profession such as "handicraftsmen" who is specialist in various crafts with inherited skills and working in family groups or as individual in village and town. Sources refer to them in terms of their caste viz. the Chamar, Julaha, Kumhar, Lohar, Mochi, Sunar, Tarkhan, Thathera and the Teli etc. Their services, however, were not regularly required. Numerically too, they formed a small proportion of the total population. The Blacksmiths, Carpenters, Weavers, Potters, Leather-workers, Utensil-makers and Goldsmiths were important not only because of their numbers but also because of the indispensability of their work to society (Sharma, 1980).

Majority of the artisans lived in the countryside serving the village society. Because of the nature of their functions and their economic subservience to the landowners, the artisans were called kamins or menials, and were universally considered socially low. Whether Muslims, Hindus or Sikhs, they were broadly treated at par with the Sudra of the Hindu Varna system. The Chamars and Mochis, however, were considered untouchables. Probably on account of the relatively 'clean' nature of their work, the castes of goldsmiths, carpenters, blacksmiths and potters were considered superior among the artisans. The Weavers were regarded as the lowest among the 'clean' caste and next only to the leather workers in social status (Bhattacharya, 1975).

The artisans of rural areas are engaged in *jajmani* system which has durable, exclusive and multiple relations between a food producing family and the families that supply them with goods and services. It is durable in that the link may be inherited on both sides of families. *Jajmani* relations were exclusive in that the farmer family is supposed to carry on such relations with only one family. These ties are multiple in that more than economic exchange is involved that is just the exchange of shares for rice or sickles for wheat (Mandelbaum, 1972).

On social occasions like marriages and births, the artisans made ritual accessories for their patrons, such as the bridal seats and tables for worship and vessels for dowry, for which they were entitled to a fixed amount known as the 'lag' and they were called 'lagis' (Johal, 1980). The landholders maintained their economic power and social superiority over the artisans by keeping them at a low economic level. The artisans barely subsisted on the meager payments received for performing various professional and non-professional services. The artisans were, in fact, subjected to all sorts of hardships and humiliations. They were beaten over trivial issues, the land-owners would not allow them to use the same cot to sit, they were not even allowed to enter the shrines of Pirs and other religious establishment on particular festivals as the agriculturists, mostly Jats would be present there (Sharma, 1980).

The artisans were expected to live within the separate residential enclosures in the village which were known according to their castes, such as the Gali-Loharan, Gali-Tarkhana, and Gali-Thathiara etc. The Chamars, however, lived away from the main village site and the residential locality was called 'Chamrali'. The area where the number of sweeper caste was large, known as the 'Thathi'. Even when the artisans understood that their low economic level and corresponding social status was because of the nature of their work, they continued to work in the same capacities because the system guaranteed them a living and also perhaps the Jats and other upper castes would not easily allow them to move outside the Sep system. Moreover, at the outset of British rule, there had been very few openings for the artisans outside the traditional relationships (Sharma, 1996).

Due to rapidly changing environment in the British Punjab, the framework of traditional relationship between the artisans and agriculturists was significantly altered. A considerable proportion of the artisans moved out of the villages. The artisans in towns and cities were apparently free from some of the constraints faced by their counterparts in rural areas. The urban artisans were broadly of two descriptions. One, the specialists who manufacture goods and articles in there specialise trade according to the requirements of their client. They used their own implements and raw material and were paid for the job. The others worked in shops and factories on daily wage basis or on contract. The implements and raw material were provided to them by their employers (Sharma, 1996). Urban artisans were known for their specialised products of cotton and woollen textiles, as well as the embroidery, dyeing and printing, besides metal, leather, silk, paper and wood work (Baden-Powell, 1872).

The skilled artisan worked in family groups or as individual or in employment under some trader. Within fifty years after annexation of Punjab in 1848, the economic activities and the condition of urban centres had begun changing. The artisan in urban areas of average size formed around 10 per cent of the total work force. In large town and cities it was still more. For instance, in Lahore in the mid-nineteenth century, those returned as carpenters, shoe-makers, leather workers and goldsmiths formed around 15 per cent of the total working population of the city (Kumar, 1983). We may safely presume that the proportion of the artisans in other urban centres like Amritsar, Jalandhar, Hoshiarpur, Batala and Sialkot that produced a variety of goods also was fairly large. The artisans lived in separate localities (mohallas) in towns and cities (Tandon, 1961).

The Origin of the Term Thathiar

Metal craftsmen in India can be divided into two broad classes, the iron-workers mainly engaged in manufacture and servicing of tools, and the brass, bronze and copper workers producing utensils (Roy, 1996). The Thathera is a person, who makes and sells vessels of copper, brass, bronze and other mixed metals. The word 'Thathera' seems to be merely the nature of an occupation. They are known by different names like Kasera, Kasar, Tamera, Tamraker or Bell metals. Their name is derived from the Sanskrit word 'tashtakara' meaning polisher. The word *thathera* represents the sound produced while hammering a utensil. According to Risley (1891), they are brazier and are also called Kasera (a brass founder) in Shahbad (c.f. Singh, 1998). The Kasera are workers in Kansa. Those working in brass are called *thatheras*, whereas those employed in smelting metals or casting moulds for vessels are known as Barawas. They do not, however, intermarry as they do in the Punjab and Benaras. (In Sherring's view 1974:321), "Thatheras are distinct from the Kaseras". Although to some extent they labour in the same metals, yet their work is of a heavier and rougher cast and embraces iron, tin and zinc as well as brass, copper and kasa. They also carve the vessels manufactured by the *kaseras*. It is very difficult to draw an exact line between the two castes; for in some respects they pursue the same calling. Nevertheless, they keep themselves entirely apart, and do not permit family alliances with one another. The Bharawa caste, he further says, "is especially engaged in the occupation of preparing moulds of various shapes and kinds for casting vessels."

Sherring *(ibid)* describes them as occupying a high position even holding a place above the vashiyas, but this is not the case in Rajasthan, where they rank on par with the other artisan castes. Widows are allowed to marry again.

The Kaseras are workers in kasa, a compound metal, and also in brass and copper, and in most other kinds of metal; including gold and silver, but excluding iron and tin. They manufacture utensils for domestic use, which in India, for the most part, are made of either copper or brass. They also, to some extent, manufacture ornaments to be worn on the person, many of which are either made entirely of one or other of these two metals or of several metals compound together. Women in Rajasthan are exceedingly fond of wearing ornaments made of beautifully white compound metal, white as silver, yet cheaper.

As artisans and traders, the Kasera caste occupies a high position. They are said to be above the Vaisya, or commercial caste, and to hold a place between this and the Kshatriya caste. The reason assigned for this opinion are, that the tribe in all its sub-divisions is more punctilious on many matters considered to be of importance by Hindu than the Vaisya or Sudra castes usually arc, and that they all wear the sacred thread. This, however, is no sufficient reason for elevating them above the Vaisyas, to which family they naturally belong. They are divided into seven clans: Purbiya, Panchhawan, Gorakhpuri, Tank, Tanchard, Bhariya and Golar. None of these intermarry or eat together. The four first sub-divisions are name given to such Kaseras as have emigrated from those parts of the country to which they refer. The Purbiyas are from the east, the Pachhawans from the west; the Gorakhpuris from the district of Gorakhpur; and the Tanks, most probably, from the principality of Tonk.

This tribe is very numerous in the city of Mirzapur, where a considerable trade is carried on in brass wares. The Kaseras manufacture all kinds of brass utensils, which are sent to distant parts of the country for sale.

According to Gahlot (1989), the Kaseras work in brass, copper and other metals with the exception of iron and tin. Like other artisans, the Kaseras also claim descent from the Rajputs. Henry Elliot (c.f. Gahlot, 1989) called them Kashera from 'Kansa', bell-metal and 'bharna' (to fill something) and describes them as forming one of the sub-divisions of the sunars. In Western Rajasthan they follow most of the customs of the Bamania-sunars.

The Kaseras worship Shakti, and wear the sacred thread, especially on the occasion of their marriage. At their feast, they also distribute Dakshina among their caste people like the Pushkarna Brahmanas. In case of adoption, the usual, ceremony of *pagri-bandhna* (turban wearing) is performed; if a near relation is adopted, only one turban is supplied to him by the family of the adoptive father, but if a remote kinsman is adopted, each member of the family has to furnish a turban separately. They also, to some extent, manufacture ornaments to be worn by women. Women in Rajasthan are fond of wearing ornaments made of white compound metal, white as silver, yet cheaper.

Myths on the Origin of the Term

As among the artisans and traders, the Thathiars claim Khatri status. There are various myths regarding their origin, one is that these people were victims of a devastating attack by Parasuram, after which they scattered all over the Ganges valley and distinguished their social reality (Blunt, 1969).

Crooke (1974) ascribes their origin to Lord Parasuram. According to a myth given by Russell and Hiralal (1975) they trace their origin from Dharampal, the son of Sahasra Arjun or Arjun of the thousand arms. Arjun was the great grandson of Eksbvaku, who was born in the forests of Kalinga, from the union of a mare and a snake. On this account, the Kasars of the Maratha region say that they all belong to the Ahihaya clan (Ahi, a snake and Haya, a mare).

Arjun was killed by Parasuram during the slaughter of the Kshatriyas and Dharampal's mother escaped with three other pregnant women. According to another version all the four women were the wives of the king of the Somvansi Rajputs who stole the sacred cow Kamdhenu. Their four sons on growing up wished to avenge their father's murder and prayed to Goddess Kali for weapons. But unfortunately in their prayer, instead of saying ban arrow they said van, which means pot, and hence brass pots were given to them instead of arrows. They set out to sell the pots, but got involved in a quarrel with a Raja, who killed three of them, but was defeated by the fourth, to whom he afterwards gave his daughter and half his kingdom, and this hero became the ancestor of the Kasars.

According to Risley (1891) they are probably an offshoot from one of the higher mercantile caste, which was separated from the parent groups by adopting this special profession. The fact that Thathiar have a well defined set of exogamous sections and pride themselves on their purity of descent seem to indicate that the caste is a homogenous one, and is not, like many of the functional castes, a collection of men from several different groups held together merely by the bond of a common occupation. In Mirzapur, which is one of the headquarters of the caste, they call themselves Kshatriyas and assert that they were driven to adopt their present occupation when Parasuram inflicted a general massacre upon the Kshatriya race (c.f. Crooke, W. 1974).

According to Russell and Hiralal (1975), the caste has a number of sub-divisions mainly of a territorial nature. Among these are the Maratha Kasars, the Deshkar, who also belong to the Maratha country, the Pardesi or foreigners, the Jhade or residents of the forest country of the central provinces and the Audhia, or Ajudhiabasi who are immigrants from Oudh. Another sub-division, the Bharewas, is of a distinctly lower status than the body of the caste, and has non-Aryan customs, such as the eating of pork.

They make the heavy brass ornaments, which the Gond and other tribes wear on their legs and are probably an occupational offshoot from one of these tribes. In Chanda, some of the Bharewas serve as grooms and are looked down upon by the others. They have totemistic septs, named after animals and plants, some of which are Gond words, and among them the bride goes to the bridegroom's house to be married, which is a Gond custom. The Bharewas may more properly be considered as a separate caste of lower status. As previously stated, the Maratha and Deshkar sub-castes of the Maratha region no longer make vessels, but only put them for sale. One sub-caste, the Otaris, make vessels from moulds, while the remainder cut and hammer into shape the imported sheets of brass. Lastly, come a group comprising those members of the caste who are of doubtful or illegitimate descent, and these are known as 'Takle'. In the Maratha region, the Kasars as already seen, say that they all belong to one *gotra*, the Ahihaya. They have, however, collections of families distinguished by different surnames and persons having the same surname are forbidden to marry. In the northern districts they have the usual collection of exogamous septs, usually names after villages.

Ibbetson (1961) remarks that until 1881 they seem to have enjoyed the rare distinction of being one of the few salt range tribes which claimed Rajput origin asserting that their original home was in Jammu and that they obtained their present territories by joining the armies of Babar. Whatever may be the thought of the claim of the kasars to rank as Mughals, they certainly have a good position amongst the tribes of the district, ranking in popular estimation with the Mairs and Kahuts. They intermarry freely with the former, both giving and taking daughters, but a Kassar of good family who married his daughter to a Kahut of fair standing incurred the displeasure of the brotherhood. They do not intermarry with any other tribe, though as is usually the case in the Jhelum district low caste wives are occasionally taken by them. Mairs, Kassars and Kahuts eat together, but not with Kamins.

It is not only the Thathiars who have evolved the myths regarding their origin and occupation rather other artisanal groups such as Chamars (Sharma, 1986), Potters (Krishnan, 1989) and Blacksmiths (Bal, 1995), have also constructed variety of myths revolving around their origin and nature of the work. All of them give a divine explanation of the origin and thus claim a higher status.

Thathiars of Different Regions

As Bal (1995) in the study of Blacksmiths as an occupational group discusses that in a linguistic cultural region, the occupation of smithy is carried over by single endogamous group. With the change in region, this endogamous group change not only in terms of nomenclature but also culturally. Thus, in Indian setting, we have regional basis of occupation in terms of who performs it.

Utensil, making is basically a broad occupation in which specific skills of different nature are required e.g., household goods, decorative and ornamental work. Tools and weapons require skills of diverse nature not necessarily the attribute of different endogamous groups.

Census actual workers in brass and bronze expanded, from about 125,000 in 1891 to 145,000 in 1901, declined in 1921 to 106,000 was 120,000 in I931, and thereafter, for three decades it remained stationary at a little over a hundred thousand. The censuses of 1971 and 1981 club these activities under 'metal products', but the overall employment figure shows no significant change. There must be only two possible explanations of this long stability consistent with our hypothesis that the market for brass did expand: (a) productivity improved in the industry via use of new technologies and work-processes, and (b) the very growth of trade created new constraints for the artisans. In fact, the aggregate employment statistics itself provides an indirect confirmation of the former. Interestingly, an unusually large component of brass-ware employment (50 per cent) in the 1961 census was 'non-household'. Already in 1921, the Industrial Census had shown that 13-14 per cent of actual workers were employees in the 300 odd factories, 260 of which did not use mechanical power. This is consistent with concentration in a number of other crafts, but the proportions are higher in brass. The proportion of non-household workers in 1961 was above average in all the major states, except Madras. It also appears, but cannot be conclusively tested without adjusting for provincial borders, that between 1931 and 1961, brass-ware employment expanded in the major provinces: Maharashtra, Gujarat, West Bengal, Uttar Pradesh, and Tamil Nadu, and declined else-where. But relative growth was smaller in the east, and employment sharply declined in the Punjab, the eastern districts of which used to be a major brass producer. At the same time, the very process of growth also carried within itself constraints, by creating need for adaptations which not everyone could meet with success. These challenges differed somewhat depending on whether the product was utilitarian or decorative, but in both, they showed up through heightened competition within the craft (Roy, 1996).

According to Census 1921, Table 2.1 indicates that total population of the Thathiars in Punjab was 4334, out of which 2342 were males and 1992 were females. Table 2.2 reveals that a large proportion of the Thathiars were mainly from Ambala (55.24%) and Lahore (25.71%) divisions. Gurgaon, Karnal and Hisar of Ambala division, which are now in Haryana, and Amritsar and Gurdaspur of Lahore division, had highest concentration of the Thathiars. Religion-wise distribution of the Thathiars of Punjab in Table 2.3 shows that 59.25 per cent were Hindus, 35.25 per cent were Muslims, 4.56 per cent were Sikhs; besides this 0.94 per cent were Buddhists.

Table 2.1
Total Population of the Thathiars of the Punjab-1921

Punjab	*Males*	*Females*	*Total*
British Territory	2023	1764	3787 (87.37)
Punjab States	319	228	547 (12.63)
Total	**2342 (54.04)**	**1992 (45.96)**	**4334 (100.00)**

Figures within parenthesis indicate percentage.

Table 2.2
Division-wise Population Distribution of the Thathiars of British Territories of Punjab in 1921

Divisions	*Males*	*Females*	*Total*
Ambala	1148	943	2091 (55.24)
Lahore	495	479	974 (25.71)
Multan	199	147	346 (9.13)
Jalandhar	100	101	201 (5.30)
Rawalpindi	81	94	175 (4.62)
Total	**2023 (53.42)**	**1764 (46.58)**	**3787 (100.00)**

Figures within parenthesis indicate percentage.

Table 2.3
Religion-wise Distribution of the Thathiars of Punjab 1921

Religion	*Males*	*Females*	*Total*
Hindu	1407	1161	2568 (59.25)
Musalman	810	718	1528 (35.25)
Sikh	105	93	198 (4.56)
Budh	20	20	40 (0.94)
Total	**2342 (54.04)**	**1992 (45.96)**	**4334 (100.00)**

Figures within parenthesis indicate percentage.

The National Scenario

The evidence of the Thathiars (Bell Metal) craft have been discovered in the relics of Mohanjodaro and Harappa civilisations, which prove the historical and traditional importance of the industry. Even today it is practiced in several parts of the country like Orissa, Madhya Pradesh, Chhattisgarh, Jharkhand, Bihar and U.P. etc. These bell metal artisans are mostly tribal people.

The metal crafts sector plays a vital role in providing employment to our rural population. In India, there are about three million handicraft artisans and most of them are working in metal sector. These metal artisans display inherent creativity and play a significant role in protecting the traditional art and culture of our nation (metalkondagaon.PDF-9327F093-eedc-4).

We may now focus on the Thathiars of different regions Singh (1998) state, that they are distributed in thirty four districts of Uttar Pradesh, Haryana, Rajasthan, Delhi and Bihar having fifty six segments.

In Uttar Pradesh, the Thathera, also known as Kasera or Tambera, are concentrated in the Lalitpur, Banda, Fatehpur, Kanpur, Lucknow and Mirzapur districts. According to the 1931 Census, the population of Thathera in the United Provinces of Agra and Oudh was 18,190. The primary occupation of the Thathera community is making copper utensils and a few families still do what community has been doing for generations.

In Haryana, the Thathera are known as Kashera, claim to have originated from the Rajput caste among the Hindus. During the Puranic period, they changed their warrior role to weapon manufacturing. Later on, they also minted coins of silver and gold. After the First War of Independence in 1857, they abandoned the occupation of manufacturing weapons and began to make utensils from various metals. They are confined to cities and towns of the state with concentration in Rewari and Bhiwani towns. Economically, the Thathera are dependent upon the supply of various kinds of metals.

In Delhi, the Thatheras are known as Kasera, Tamera or Kansor. They trace their origin to Dharmpal, the son of Sahastra Arjun who was killed by Parashuram when he set out to destroy the Kshatriya. The Thatheras have a number of endogamous sub-divisions and their differentiation is based on territorial level. There are fifty two *gotras* among the Thathiars. They are traditionally engaged in making metallic vessels, ornaments and ornamental figures from copper, brass and bell metals with artistic carvings on them (Singh, 1998).

In Bihar, the Thatheras are referred to as Tamrakar or Thatheri; they are distributed in the districts of Patna, Nalanda, Gaya, Nawada, Bhagalpur, Ranchi, Muzaffarpur etc. The Indo-Aryan language Magahi is spoken at home. They are conversant with Hindi also. They have a number of exogamous groups called Parich. Their traditional surnames are Sao, Ram, Thathera, and Thatheri etc. while the surnames recently adopted are Gupta, Prasad, Sinha, Sah etc., they have only one *gotra*, i.e., Kasyap. They practice endogamy at the community and *gotra* levels and exogamy at the parich and village levels. The traditional occupation of the Thathera is sale and repair of utensils. They are also engaged in business and services. Pounia or Jajmani relationship exists with the Brahmin, Nai, Mali, and Chamar etc.

The most important of the North-Western provincial brass and copper manufactures are, however, the Benares brass ware, the Moradabad brass ware and Lucknow copper vessels. All these three manufactures have advanced in rapid strides into European favour during the last few years, and at present no dealer in Indian art manufactures considers his stock-in-trade complete without a good collection of these articles, especially of the first two.

At Jagadhri in the Ambala district, lamps and cooking utensils of all sorts are largely made. Some of these are exceptionally well executed, specially the lamps, with branching arms touched with colours on the leaves (Mukherji, 1974).

During 1947 partition, bulk of the departing urban Muslim population of the east Punjab, consisted of artisans, mechanics, craftsmen, blacksmith, potters, butchers and the like, while the vast majority of urban Hindu and Sikh refugees from west Pakistan belonged to the trading classes. Economically, it was a diffi cult situation. These people could not take to their original professions because their scope was limited and they could not take to vocations left by the Muslims as they did not have the required skills (Rai, 1986).

According to government estimates nearly 18,54,188 Muslims, belonging to 22 different artisans migrated to Pakistan. The non-Muslims artisan who migrated to east Punjab numbered 2,52,873. This left a tremendous gap in the occupations. The government estimated that in order to fill this gap, they required about 40,000 weavers, 15,000 potters an equivalent number of blacksmiths, Telis (oil extractors) and leather workers about 10,000 barbers, another10,000 carpenters, 10 to 15 thousand butchers and three to four thousand tailors.(c.f. Rai,1986).

The immediate problem before the government was, therefore, to save the life of the province from complete paralysis. This, obviously, meant that the large populace of shop-keepers and hawkers should be diverted towards skilled labour and other such vocations. In order to fill the gap six vocational centres were started all over the province. The trainees were encouraged to manufacture saleable goods which were put on sale in depots opened for the purpose. Industry department in addition maintained 23 industrial schools and no demonstration parties (Rai, 1986).

In these training centres instructions were given in the following trades, carpentry, blacksmithy, brick-laying, metal moulding, general electrical and mechanical vocations, pattern making, watch repairing, turnership, hand-weaving, wood-turning and the like.

The partition of Punjab facilitated the growth of certain industries in the province, for instance industrialists of Gujranwala dealing in brass, after migration to the Punjab installed 15 brass-rolling mills and 94 brass utensil making factories. This added to the already existing 11 brass-rolling mills and two brass utensil making concerns at Jagadhari (Kashyap, 1957).

In the Punjab, brass articles are manufactured in almost all the major cities like Amritsar, Ambala, Ludhiana, Jalandhar, Gurdaspur and Hoshiarpur. Earlier brass vessels were exported to the hills around the Punjab and up the Kabul valley into Afghanistan. In every large town, great qualities of metal vessels, drinking cups, cooking pots, lamps and all articles of household use, are made for local consumption. Copper vessels engraved and tinned are made at Amritsar. These are in the Kashmiri style. In short, the industry is introduced by a colony of Kashmiris settled in this town. At Phagwara, plain brass work of excellent finish and character is largely manufactured. Plates, cups and other articles made here are exported to various parts of Punjab. At Bhadurpur, near Hoshiarpur, brass vessels are largely made and exported to the hills. It is said that they find their way as far as Ladakh. The finish is exceptionally good (Mukherji, 1974).

Social Practices

Among the Thathiars of Uttar Pradesh, Rajasthan and Benaras, infant marriage was the rule with all the more respectable Kaseras, but ordinary people marry their daughters at ten or twelve. Inter-tribal fornication in the cases of unmarried people or widows and widowers seems to be lightly regarded. In Bihar, it would seem that polygamy is allowed only if the first wife is barren: here, as far as can be ascertained, a man may marry as many wives as he can afford to keep. They have the ordinary forms of marriage Charhauwa, the respectable form, *dola* used by poor people. Widows can marry by *sagai*, but they profess this to be a modern institution. She may marry the younger brother of her late husband or an outsider as she pleases. A husband can put away his wife for adultery with a member of another caste, and a wife, can leave her husband if he does not support her, or abandons his religion. Divorced women cannot remarry within the tribe (Crooke, 1974).

At Ratanpur, in Mandla on Amawas or the day of the new moon of Phagun (February), every Kasar must return to the community of which he is a member and celebrate the feast with them. And in default of this, he will be expelled from caste until the next Amawas of Phagun (Feb-March) comes around. They close their shops and worship the implements of their trade on this day. The Kasars, as already stated rank next to the sunars among the artisan castes, and the Audhia sunars who make ornaments of bell metals, form a connecting link between the two groups. The social status of the Kasars varies in different localities. In some places Brahmins take water from them but not in others. Some Kasars now invest boys with the sacred thread at their weddings, and thereafter it is regularly worn (Russell and Hiralal, 1975).

Religious Practices

The information collected through various secondary sources reveals that majority of persons of this caste are Hindus and Sikhs. Hindus and most of the Sikhs worship the Goddess Singhbahami or Devi riding on a tiger. They make an image of her in the most expensive metal; they can afford, and worship it daily. Kaseras generally follow the Vaishnava or Nanakpanthi sect. Their clan deities are the Panchonpir Durga, and Bandi Devi. These are worshipped in the month of Jeth (May) on a Sunday or Wednesday, with offerings of pulse cake (Phulauri) and bread. Durga is worshipped on 15th Chait (March) with an offering of cakes (Puri), Khir and sweetmeats. Bandi Devi is honoured with an offering of pepper and sugar dissolved in water at the full moon of Sawan. When a person recovers from small-pox, a yellow cloth and some flowers are dedicated to Sitala Mata. All these offerings are after dedication, consumed by the worshippers. Their priests are Tiwari Brahmins, who are received on terms of equality by other Brahmins. They worship their trade implements on the day of the new moon in Chait (March) and Bhadon (August). A trident as a symbol of Devi, is then drawn with powdered rice and vermilion on the furnace and coconut is broken and distributed to the caste fellows, no outsider being allowed to be present. They quench their furnace on the new moon day of every month. The Ramnaumi and Durgapuja or nine days fasts in the months of Chait (March) and Asu (October) and for the two days, following the Diwali and Holi festivals. On these days, they will not prepare any new vessels, but will sell those which they have ready. The Tameras have Kanaujia Brahmins for their priests and the Brahmins will take food from them which have been cooked without water and salt. On this account other Kanaujia Brahmins require a heavy payment. The caste abstains from liquor and some of them have abjured all flesh food while others partake of it. They usually wear the sacred thread. Brahmins will take water from their hands and the menial caste will eat food which they have touched (Crooke, 1974).

The dead are cremated in the ordinary way, and *balis* (Pinda) are offered to them on the 15th of any month, which falls on a Wednesday. On such occasions, uncooked grains are given to Brahmins. People who die in a distant land or who have died a violent death are thrown into running water and cremated in effigy, with the usual ceremonies, within the six months of death. These religious practices are performed, mostly in all regions i.e. Uttar Pradesh, Bihar, Haryana, Delhi, Punjab etc. (Crooke, 1974).

Nature of the Work

In the different parts of the country, this caste group is found making utensils of all kinds for eating and drinking vessels, ornaments and ornamental figures from brass, copper and bell metal. Brass is the metal most in favour for utensils and it is usually imported in sheets from Bombay, but in places it is manufactured from a mixture of three parts of copper and two parts of zinc. This is considered the best brass, though it is not as hard as the inferior kinds, in which the proportion of zinc is increased. Ornaments of a grey colour, intended to resemble silver, are made from a mixture of four parts of copper with five parts of zinc. Bell metal is an alloy of copper and tin, and in Chanda is made of four parts of copper to one part tin or tinfoil, the tin being the more expensive metal. Bells of fairly good size and excellent tone are moulded from this amalgam, and plates or saucers in which anything acidic in the way of food is to be kept are also made of it, since acids do not rust this metal as they do brass and copper. But bell metal vessels are fragile and sometimes break when dropped. They cannot also be heated on the fire to clean them and therefore cannot be lent to persons outside the family, while brass vessels may be lent to friends of other castes, and on being received back pollution is removed by heating them on the fire or placing hot ashes in them. Brahmins make a small fire of grass for this purpose and pass the vessels through the flame. Copper cooking pots are commonly used by Muhammadans but not by Hindus, as they have to be coated with tin, the Hindus consider that tin is an inferior metal whose application to copper degrades the latter. Pots made of brass with a copper rim are called 'Ganga Jamni' after the confluence of the dark water of the Jamuna with the muddy stream of the Ganges, whose union they are supposed to symbolise. Small figures of the deities or idols are also made of brass, but some Kasars will not attempt this work, because they are afraid of the displeasure of the God in case the figure should not be well or symmetrically shaped (Russell and Hiralal, 1975).

There is some difference of opinion as to their occupation. According to Nesfield (1983, 202), "The Kasera's speciality lies in mixing the softer metal (zinc, copper and tin) and moulding the alloy into various shapes, such as cups, bowls, plates etc. The Thatheras art consists in polishing and engraving the utensils which the Kasera supplies." On the other hand, Hoey writes that at Lucknow the manufacturer of brass vessels is called indifferently Thathera, Kasera or Bhariya. In Mirzapur, it appears that the name Kasera is confined to the moulder of vessels in brass or alloy and to the man who beats out trays out of metal sheets, while the Thathera makes and sells ornaments made of alloy (c.f. Crooke, 1974).

Thathiars of Jandiala Guru

This town is famous for utensil making. There is numerically preponderant number of population engaged in this work. There is considerable manufacturing of plain brass wares and is exported on a large scale. For this manufacturing activity, town has a good name. There are six wards, where Thathiars have their work or residential places. Work has been divided into various categories like manufacturing, contractual, selling and traditional artisanal work. Diversification and modification took place in the work processes from time to time. Most of the traditional artisans have moved away from this work and joined factories as skilled workers. The changes in the occupational structure of Thathiars introduced transformation in their social and economic spheres. Traditional Thathiars are considered of backward caste in the caste hierarchy. But those who are in high status jobs related with utensil making, they mention themselves as Khatri by caste. For the purpose of research, the myths of the Thathiars were collected from the respondents. It is interesting to find out that most of the myths revolve around their origin. They claim that their origin is from Parasuram, as they have listened from their forefathers. He was a king of the community. Even now, they worship Parasuram. They perform some rituals on Parasuram Jayanti. They observe fast in which they wear yellow thread on the arm and they worship berry tree on this day. Some describe origin by Vishkarma. The legendary Vishkarma, a son of Brahmin is regarded as the divine *shilpi* (skillful) who imparted training to mankind in all sorts of manual work, skills, trades and arts. He taught men architecture; work in stone, clay, wood, metal, leather etc. Some said, it is a part of mercantile community. Another myth described that their origin is from Shivji. He once said to a person to prepare a 'Trishule' of brass. The person pretended him again and again. After the wait for a long period, he went to that person and said him to mark the figure of 'Trishule' on the earth. That person did it, and then he asked him to pick up this figure (Trishule) which was ready. Shivji said, these words to that person 'Tu hamesha thadha (thaa-thaa) hi karta rahega' (you will always remain busy in making noise). From that day Thathiars took their name from Shivji.

All these myths ascribe the origin of the Thathiars. Myths are stories. These narrate a series of events. But their significance for Levi-Strauss (1977) can only be revealed by bringing out their underlying a temporal structure. The process of decomposing the myths involved reducing the text to sentences or 'my themes'. Each of these my theme is a relation and has to be combined with others to produce 'bundle' of relations which will show up the patterns of logical connection and transformation. The means of decomposing them is, in the first instance, the notion of 'binary opposition', the linguistic technique of identifying things in terms of their contrastive values, such as 'has/ does not have', 'up-down' and so on. Myths are layered. A single myth states a message several times in different ways (c.f. Sharrock, *et.al*, 2003).

Like the myths of Asdiwal, myths of the Thathiars show some variations. As they were born in the forest of Kalinga but their original place is called Ratanpur. From sociological consideration it shows structure like this at the beginning it involves son, father and great grandson, in the middle mother and son and at the end, father, son and daughter. Another variation shows the avenging of son against father, they need ban-arrow, in their prayer, instead of saying ban-arrow they said van which means pot and hence brass pots were given to them instead of arrows.

On the other hand, stories about the caste of the Thathiars narrate that in Mirzapur, which is one of the headquarters of the caste, they call themselves Kshatriya and assert that they were driven to adopt their present occupation when Parasuram made a general massacre of the Kshatriya race (Crooke, 1974).

But, on the other side, information collected from the Thathiars of Jandiala Guru reveals that after Independence, they were identified as 'backward caste' because their occupation is of lower status, involves manual work and earnings were less. They got themselves registered as backward caste. So that they could get certain reserved quotas of raw material, reservation in government services, scholarship for study of children from government as backward caste. But with the transformation in their occupation, many of them have become manufacturers, contractors, wholesalers, retailers and skilled workers. Due to this change in work pattern, they started considering themselves as Khatris. Since, they now have taken the occupation of Khatris, i.e., the trade and commercial activities; therefore, over the time they have evolved various myths regarding the origin of their caste and started identifying themselves as Khatris.

To sum up, we can mention that the Thathiars are urban artisans, Risely, Sherring and others described about the origin of the term Thathiar. The word 'Thathera' deal with nature of an occupation. Various myths on the origin of the Thathiars, which relate with various deities, have been discussed. Thathiars of other regions, i.e., Uttar Pradesh, Haryana, Rajasthan, Delhi, Bihar and Punjab, their social customs, religion and occupation have been explored. The Thathiars of Jandiala Guru have also evolved various myths about their origin. These myths narrate a series of events. The analysis of these myths according to Levi-Strauss shows a comparative relationship between various events of myths.

3

Socio-economic Profile of Thathiars

In the previous chapter, attention has been given to the Thathiars as an artisan caste group. The origin of the term Thathiar and myths regarding the origin of the term have been discussed. These myths have been found to be still an integral part of this occupation. Since most of the myths are associated with the origin and other related aspects of the Thathiar caste. Another description was about the Thathiars of other regions, besides their social customs, religion and occupation. However, the main focus was on the Thathiars of Jandiala Guru.

Aristotle, the Greek philosopher who was speaking about physics, said, there and elsewhere we shall not obtain the best insight into the things until we actually see them growing from beginnings (c.f. Wadhawan, 1972). For the proper understanding of the socio-economic background of the Thathiars, we need to define the elastic term social background. Its constituents vary from situation to situation and from time to time. The social background of a person affects his social behaviour, attitudes, prejudices, nature etc. Social status generally coincides with economic status. It is difficult to discern a definite pattern in which social change results directly from technological development, continuous technological change may alter the structure of the society itself. Therefore, the analysis is necessary to relate the cause of human action to their socio-economic characteristics. The role played by these traits is equally important in causing a social action.

In this chapter an attempt has been made to analyse certain socio-economic variables such as age, marital status, religion, caste, education, family size and migration pattern of the Thathiars.

Age

Age reveals the levels of maturity and fixation of the ideas, custom, sanctions etc. In traditional societies like that of India, aged persons are honoured and ranked higher than the younger ones. On the ladder of social stratification, the mature age also has a prestige which exhibits itself differently in various occupational pursuits. Age is a badge of experience and maturity of age gives certain advantages in many occupational pursuits. These advantages tend to stabilise career patterns of workers. Age also acts in a negative way to halt occupational mobility. Conservatism often increases with age and is a psychological block which may reduce the willingness of a worker to adapt to

Table 3.1
Age Distribution of the Respondents

Age (in years)	*Number*	*Percentage*
11 to 20	21	7.00
21 to 30	93	31.00
31 to 40	80	26.67
41 to 50	44	14.67
51 to 60	50	16.66
61 to 70	12	4.00
Total	**300**	**100.00**

a different work position and to assume new habits and risk (Miller and Form, 1980). Age has a prestige which exhibits itself differently in various occupational pursuits. Young men and women may have unusual opportunities in a rapidly changing field of economic activity. New enterprises may open new channels for them. However, the upper levels of administration are not usually open to young men and women (Bal, 1995). It is essential to know the age composition of the Thathiars as it would reveal the trend in their desire to join various levels of occupation in addition to other factors.

Table 3.1 shows that most of the Thathiars join the work at an early age. The bulk of the working Thathiars, that is, 31 per cent fall in the age group of 21 to 30 years. The data also indicate that only four per cent working Thathiars are in the age category of 61 to 70 years. This is due to the fact that in old age it is difficult to put physical labour. A few, i.e., seven per cent Thathiars are below the age of 20 years, which shows that the young persons are not much interested in this occupation. Due to the change in occupational structure less number of young person's would be found in this occupation.

Marital Status

Marriage is one of the deepest and most complex web of human relations. It is the most essential part of society and social system as well. Radhakrishnan (1956) writes, "Marriage is not a mere convention but an implicit condition of human society. It is an adjustment between the biological purposes of nature and the sociological purposes of man." Marriage has been more recently defined as a legally binding contract between a man and a woman that conveys certain rights and privileges including sexual exclusivity, legitimating of any children born of the union, and economic responsibilities (c.f. Ratra, *et.al.*, 2006). As it is evident from Table 3.2, 91.6 per cent of respondents are married, 4.3 per cent respondents are unmarried, 1.6 per cent are divorced and 2.3 per cent are widows.

Table 3.2
Marital Status of the Respondents

Marital Status	*Number*	*Percentage*
Married	275	91.66
Unmarried	13	4.34
Divorced	05	1.66
Widow	07	2.34
Total	**300**	**100.00**

Religion

Anthropologists define religion as the system of social interaction consisting of those beliefs and activities that order human life by relating humans to spiritual being and or powers. Religion is an institutionalised or traditional path to salvation. From a Marxian perspective, religion as a part of the superstructure of society is shaped ultimately by the infrastructure. Thus, changes in the forces of production will be mirrored by changes in religious beliefs and practices. Max Weber rejects the view that religion is always shaped by economic factors. He does not deny that at certain times and in certain places, religious behaviour may be largely shaped by economic forces, but he maintains that this is not always the case. Under certain conditions, the reverse can occur, that is, religious beliefs can be a major influence on economic behaviour. Religious composition of the town indicates that there are (49.3 per cent) Sikhs, (46.6 per cent) Hindus, (3.6 per cent) Jains and (0.3 per cent) are Muslims.

Table 3.3
Religion of the Respondents

Religion	*Number*	*Percentage*
Sikh	161	53.66
Hindu	139	46.34
Total	**300**	**100.00**

Data indicate that 161 (53.66 per cent) Thathiars are Sikhs and 139 (46.34 per cent) are Hindus. Mainly there are two religions–Hindu and Sikh–who are engaged in utensil making occupation.

Caste

Caste in Indian context is a status group which defines the social and ritual position of an individual in the society. It is defined as a relatively small and named group of persons characterised by hereditary membership, endogamy and a specific style of life which also include the pursuit by tradition of a particular occupation and is usually associated with an hierarchical order (Betteille, 1971). According to the principles of traditional caste system, each caste has hereditary occupation. The occupation of a person is determined by his birth in the caste. Under the impact of industrialisation and urbanisation occupations are undergoing radical transformation (Judge and Bal, 2006). It has been argued by sociologists and social anthropologists that caste system is an exclusive feature of Indian social structure. The greatest change in the caste system probably occurred in relation to the occupational structure, i.e., caste and occupation. This study depicts that all the 300 respondents belong to Khatri caste. The Thathiars, who were traditional artisans, have changed their caste. They got themselves registered as backward caste because of poor working conditions. With the passage of time they have moved away from traditional Thathiar work and joined other occupations in utensil making, i.e., manufacturers, contractors, wholesalers, retailers and skilled workers. Most of the traditional Thathiars have joined as skilled workers in small-scale factories and workshops. This change in their work made them economically better off than before. This change in occupation brought change in caste status; hence they started claiming a Khatri caste status. Khatris consider themselves to be Kshatriyas. Khatris of Punjab are a small but one of the most successful communities in contemporary

India. They are prominent in all fields of activity–politics, arts, entertainment, industry, trade, hotels, army and bureaucracy (www.chowk.com).

Education

Education is a key that opens that door in life which is essentially social in character and plays a very significant role to determine one's socio-economic status. Education is of such nature which control external behaviour of man as well as internal motives, impulses and attitudes. According to Ruskin, 'Education consists making people polite, teaching, what they ought to be. Hence, education opens up new job avenues for the people. Educated individuals are more exposed to modern ideas which provide them with a new kind of awareness of the existing social set up. Education provides them consciousness as well as opportunities to come out of their existing traditional bonds of occupation and to make a choice of a new occupation. It provides them the opportunities to move in the social hierarchy which consequently make the social structure less rigid.

Table 3.4
Educational Level of Respondents

Education	*Number*	*Percentage*
Illiterate	43	14.34
Upto Primary	61	20.34
Middle	72	24.00
Metric	53	17.66
+2/Higher Secondary	39	13.00
Graduate	23	7.66
Post-Graduate	09	3.00
Total	**300**	**100.00**

Educational level of the Thathiars has been shown in Table 3.4, it reveals that 14.34 per cent are illiterate,

20.34 per cent acquired education upto primary, 24 per cent have got education only upto middle, 17.66 per cent have upto metric, 13 per cent acquired education upto higher secondary and 7.66 per cent have passed graduation. Only three per cent have gone in for higher education. Data indicate that none of them has received the technical quali cations, but they are capable of doing their work with great expertise and skill.

Occupation

A set of activities centred on an economic role are usually associated with earning a living, for instance, a trade or an occupation. An occupation is a social role that is determined by the general division of labour within a society. As a specialisation of an individual function in society, it is important factor de ning a person's prestige, class position and style of life.

Table 3.5
Occupation of the Respondents

Occupation	*Number*	*Percentage*
Traditional Thathiars	80	26.66
Manufacturers	17	05.66
Manufacturers-cum-Contractors	16	05.34
Wholesalers of utensils	9	03.00
Shopkeepers of utensils raw/waste material	4	01.34
Contractors-cum-shopkeepers of utensils	28	09.34
Contractors	23	07.66
Retail shopkeepers of utensils	26	08.66
Skilled workers	97	32.34
Total	**300**	**100.00**

In the Indian society, the caste is considered to be characterised by hereditary occupation. Notwithstanding the negative aspects of this system, in a way, it has been relatively easier to perform the hereditary occupation than in shift on to some other occupation. Occupation plays important role in individual's life. In modern period, with the advent of industries and increasing competition, the occupational structure of society has undergone transformation where more emphasis is given to one's own capabilities and education.

Data in Table 3.5 reveal that a large proportion (26.66 per cent) of respondents are traditional Thathiars and skilled workers are (32.34 per cent). Traditional Thathiars are still using their traditional tools along with the use of modern machines. Industrialisation and transformation give rise to other jobs in utensil making. Manufacturers are running independent processing units, i.e., small-scale factories. They supervise the whole production process. Beside this, 5.34 per cent manufacturers are engaged in combined activity of manufacturer-cum-contractor. They arrange contract with skilled workers and traditional Thathiars. Wholesalers of utensils mainly sell the products in bulk quantity to the retailers. Some shops are of raw/waste material. Another type of diversification in the work is of contractor-cum-shopkeeper (9.34 per cent) of utensils. In this they fix contract with workers to produce the goods. After getting ready material, they sell the products directly to the local market. Contractor mainly works with traditional Thathiars and skilled workers. With the mechanisation of traditional work, many people got displaced from work who later became skilled workers in the small-scale factories or workshops.

Household Information

Household means all persons who live in the same dwelling unit. The dwelling unit may be a house, an apartment or a group of rooms or a room. According to census de□nition, a household includes not only family members but also persons who are not related to each other, if they share the same dwelling unit. A person living alone is also considered a household.

The families with husband, wife and children are 19.34 per cent. Respondent, wife, children, uncle, brother and sister households are 17.66 per cent. Households with respondent, wife, children and mother, father relationship are 16.34 per cent. Respondent, wife, children, married brother and unmarried brother and sister households are 14.34 per cent. Households like respondent, wife, children, mother, father and brother and sister relationship are 12.34 per cent. In the case of respondent, wife, one parent and brother, sister households are 10.66 per cent. Only 9.32 per cent households are of respondent, wife, married or unmarried children and grand-children.

Family Type

Family has been seen as a universal social institution and inevitable for human society. By family structure we mean a group of persons of both sexes related by marriage, blood or adoption, performing roles based on age, sex and relationship characterised by common residence, economic cooperation and reproduction (Ahuja, 1993). Sociologically it is one of the most important variables. Family performs various functions, such as biological–reproduction, food, housing and clothing; psychological–affection, love, security, protection and care, economic–division of labour, arrangement of income, organisation and care of property, social function–to establish status, socialisation, social control, assistance in choice of partner; religious, cultural, and educational functions (Ratra, *et.al.*, 2006). The respondents reside in all the three types namely, nuclear, extended and joint families. The nuclear family consists of husband, wife and their unmarried children. Extended family is that family in which husband, wife and their unmarried children and a single member from either husband's or wife's side resides.

Joint family household means a typical three generational family or at least two couples with or without their married or unmarried children.

Data reveal that 19.34 per cent respondents are living in nuclear families. Mostly those persons are having nuclear family that had migrated from Pakistan or other places. There are 34.00 per cent respondents who are living in extended families. The respondents who are living in joint family are 46.66 per cent. Since they work in familial setting, the family remains the production as well as the consumption unit. In joint families, the head of the household remains the main representative in the work setting. He gets help in raising capital, managerial support, and organisational skill from his family.

Place of Residence

A house or residence can be defined as the physical structure where a family lives. In the primitive ages, people used to live in caves to protect themselves from heat, light, rain, dust and wild animals. Today a house is not simply a place providing shelter to people or protecting them from natural calamities, but it also gives them a feeling of security and satisfaction. Type of living shows the economic background of the workers. A man's economic background can be judged easily from the condition of his house or the locality where he is living.

Our data show most of the workers living near the work places. The entire residential area of the town is divided into 13 wards, out of which six wards have high concentration of working Thathiars. The five wards i.e., 13, 8, 1, 12 and 10 have residences in which most of the Thathiars live. Gali Kashmirian which is ward 13, 30.66 per cent Thathiars are living there. In Thathiara Wala Bazaar ward 12, twenty five per cent Thathiars have their residences. Mori Gate ward 1 has 22 per cent residences of Thathiars. Sardaran Wali Gali ward 10 has 14.66 per cent of Thathiar residences.

Bagh Wala Khu Road, ward 8 which is an outskirt area has 6.34 per cent residences. Beside this, 1.34 per cent respondents have residences in nearby villages.

Most of the workers' families just have one or two rooms and do not have kitchen, water and toilet facilities. Houses are an uncemented or kachha houses. The residents have to face many problems regarding electricity, water supply etc.

Place of Work

Earlier, the family, primarily a consumption unit, had always been a work group, partly because the struggle for subsistence was usually beyond the capacity of individual alone and partly because for family survival, adults had to stay together for the sustenance and protection of the young (Anderson, 1964).On the one hand, industrialisation separates the place of work from the place of residence, and in doing so it pulls parents apart from children and husbands from wives. It breaks up the continuity of the traditional family. On the other hand, some other responses of the respondents, too, reveal the reasons for changing the place of work to improve <U+FFFD>nancial position. These are as follows: to expand the business, due to change in the nature of work, due to the division of property or family, to attract more customers, to work in better conditions.

For the purpose of convenience location of work has been divided into two parts: those who are doing work outside the house and those who are doing work at home. This study shows that 39.66 per cent Thathiars having their work places in Thathiara Wala Bazaar, which is central place of work. Other 23.34 per cent are working in Gali Kashmirian, 13.34 per cent have their shops at Shekh Fatha Gate, and 11.34 per cent Thathiar shops are on the Mori Gate side. Only six per cent are working in Sardaran Wali Gali, while 6.32 per cent are those who work in the house itself.

Migration

The term 'migration' means settlement or shifting of an individual or a group of individuals from one cultural area or physical space to another, more or less permanently. The term 'migration' is reserved for those changes of residence that involve a complete change and readjustment of the community affiliation of the individual. According to Durkheim (1933) in the early stages of social growth, migration has been the foremost factor in the development of division of labour and the specialisation of function (c.f. Joshi, 1989). Labour migration has been an integral and vital part of human development. In fact, the history of population migration is as old as man itself. Labour migration may be defined as a form of labour mobility towards districts or states or outside where industry and employment are expanding. In other words, migration may be the phenomenon of the flow of people over shorter or longer distances from one region to a destination either for temporary or permanent settlement (Tripathy and Dash, 1997). The search for livelihood, physical and economic security, as well as a better quality of life can be said to be major factors driving migration, both within countries and across national frontiers. Out of the total 300 respondents, 51.37per cent were born at the same place that is, Jandiala Guru. Other 47.32 per cent are migrants from Delhi, Jagadhri and Western Punjab that became part of Pakistan after partition. Out of these 15.45 per cent are from Delhi and Jagadhri and 31.87 are from Pakistan due to Indo-Pak partition, i.e., Gujaranwala, Rawalpindi, Maksuda, Islamabad and Gujarkala. Information was also collected from the Thathiars about the reasons for their migration. A proportion of 31.87 per cent respondents had to migrate due to Indo-Pak partition in 1947. Other 15.45 per cent have migrated either in search of job or to establish business in this town, because Jandiala Guru is a major market of utensil making and selling and they shifted because of relatives.

Commuters

In order to collect information about commuters, they were asked regarding the place from where they commute, mode of commuting and about their intentions to settle at the place of work. A very small number of, only four persons, which is 1.34 per cent of the total population are commuters who commute from nearby villages. Two from Devidas Pura to Jandiala Guru which is three kilometers and two from Bundala to Jandiala Guru which is five kilometers. They have their own conveyance, i.e., bicycle and scooter to come to the work places. The reasons for their commuting are mainly economic as in this town enough opportunities of work and business are available. They do not wish to settle at the place of work as their native places are quite near to the work place.

To sum up, we can say that majority of the respondents fall in the age group of 21 to 30, most of them joined the work at an early age. An overwhelming majority of respondents are married and they largely belong to Hindu and Sikh religions. Data reveal that all the 300 respondents belong to Khatri caste. A large number of respondents are educated upto primary or middle standards. Occupation of the respondents shows that a large majority of the respondents has joined as skilled workers in small-scale factories or workshops. Most of them have been living in joint and extended families. A large proportion migrated from various places, within country and from Pakistan. A very small proportion commutes to their work places from the nearby villages.

4

Changes in the Caste System

In the foregoing chapter, discussion was on the socio-economic background of the Thathiars. Every factor such as cultural, economic, demographic and technology undergoes change in the society. Among these, in modern times the technological invention is one of the important factors in explaining the social change. Due to the impact of technological development on the structure of society, we may expect that some changes might have taken place in the life of the Thathiars. For this, some variables like age, marital status, religion, caste, education, occupation etc. have been analysed.

Among these, caste is the most overwhelming factor in Indian life. Those who deny it in principle accept it in practice. Life moves within the frontiers of caste and cultured men speak in soft tones against the caste system, while its rejection in action just does not occur to them (Lohia, 1964). When thinking of India, it is hard not to think of caste. In comparative sociology and in common parlance alike, caste has become a central symbol for India, indexing it as fundamentally different from other places as well as expressing its essence. Caste defines the core of Indian tradition and it is seen today as the major threat to Indian modernity (Dirks, 2002). The spirit of caste unites the three tendencies: repulsion, hierarchy and hereditary specialisation. All three must be born in mind if one wishes to give a complete definition of caste system (Gupta, 1991).

Caste system in India is generally related to the occupational pattern of different population groups. A caste or a group of allied castes generally considers some of the callings as their hereditary occupations and there is a common notion that these occupations are sanctioned by Hindu scriptures and to give up one in pursuit of another is considered improper. But if we look back to ancient India, we find that in the Vedic period such restrictions did not exist. In a hymn of Rig-veda, we find that a man is a poet, but his father is a doctor while his mother is a grinder of corn (Sarkar, 1984).

In the Rig-veda, the earliest literature, three classes of society are very frequently mentioned and named Brahma, Kshatra and Vis. The first two represented broadly the two professions of the poet-priest and the warrior chief respectively. It is only in one of the later hymns, the celebrated Purushasukta that a reference has been made to four orders of society as emanating from the sacrifice of the primeval being. The name of those four orders are given there as Brahmana, Rajanya, Vaishya and Sudra who are said to have come respectively from the mouth, the arms, the thighs and the feet of the Creator (Ghurye, 1969).

Historically, the caste system in India has consisted of thousands of endogamous groups called *jatis*. All the *jatis* were clubbed under the varnas categories during the British colonial census of 1901. The term Varna (theoretical classification based on occupation) and *jati* (caste) are two distinct concepts: while Varna is the idealised four parts division envisaged by the above described, Twice-Born, *jati* refers to thousands of actual endogamous groups prevalent across the sub-continent. A *jati* may be divided into exogamous groups based on same *gotras* (en.wikipedia.org/wiki/caste).

The people thus consisting of four varnas and four orders of religious life would keep to their respective duties and occupations, only when they were governed by the king with his sceptre. A few Kashatriya kings became Brahmins and a few Brahmins became Kshatriya because of their changed vocations. Even at a very early date we find Brahmins practicing a lower profession. Brahmins of those days, as of these, were compelled, because of economic pressure, to work as artisans and craftsmen. Even a man of an inferior caste could employ as a hired servant a man of a higher caste. Wealth conferred dignity while poverty took it away (Sarkar, 1984).

Caste units in an area form a hierarchical order is known to be a fundamental feature of the caste system. Sociological as well as historical research since the 1950s has shown that this hierarchy was not immutable even in the pre-modern times and that its mutability has increased in the modern times. By and large, while the Brahmans were accepted as occupying the highest status and the Scavengers the lowest, there was considerable flexibility about the status of castes between these two ends. This flexibility has two dimensions: firstly, the status of a caste might change over a period of time, and the status of different sections of the same caste as a horizontal unit might differ in different territorial contexts. Secondly, there could be a juxtaposition rather than hierarchy, i.e., a concern for being different rather than being unequal, between sub-divisions within a horizontal unit. Such juxtapositions were a significant feature of caste in urban centres. This concern for juxtaposition has spread gradually in modern times, affecting even the larger castes and rural areas (Shah, 2010).

Some scholars are of the opinion that it is occupation out of which caste system sprang up. According to a theory of Slater, 'Caste' arose in India before the Aryan invasion as a result of occupations becoming hereditary and marriage being arranged by parents within the society of the common craft because sexual maturity was early and trade secrets were thus preserved. As a result of magic and religious ceremonies, exclusive occupational groups were built up (Hutton, 1951). The idea of purity and pollution related to caste and occupation has been stressed by Ketkar (1979) who points out that the chief principle on which the entire system depends is that of purity and pollution (c.f. Sarkar,1984).

But with the advent of British rule in India things changed. Caste no longer rigidly determines individual's occupation, but continues to prescribe almost in its old rigour the circle into which one has to marry. Even the apex of the ancient scheme, the priesthood of the Brahmin, which has been the great bond of social solidarity in this finely divided society, is being loosened by caste after caste (Sarkar, 1984).

Studies have shown occupational mobility amongst various caste groups. Lakshmana (1973) has highlighted certain changes that had taken place in different castes following different occupations. Varied occupational affiliations of caste as main or as subsidiary indicate that 'Caste even in rural areas are not very rigid in following the traditional occupations as it is generally supposed to be'. Thus, occupational mobility among the castes seem to be a settled fact, although it may not be of any outstanding proportion and it is undoubtedly a healthy development because it is a positive indication of the fact that Hindu society is gradually losing its proverbial immobility and moving into the direction of openness.

On the basis of his data Dube (1977) also concludes that the caste system is not an impediment in occupational changes and even before the advent of modern education, people engaged in occupations other than their caste occupations. In the study conducted by Dube, only a few respondents have mentioned their caste occupation (including agricultural labour) as their traditional occupation. Thus, deviance from the caste occupations is not solely the outcome of the impact of modern forces, but rather is rooted in the traditional system itself. Data also indicated that the caste system has not offered equal opportunities to all members of society. The low castes were relatively deprived of educational, social and economic opportunities that are the basic conditions of social mobility.

According to Srinivas (1972) the new opportunities–educational, economic, and political–were in theory of caste free; that is, they were open to all and no one was banned from having access to them by reason of birth in a particular caste, sect or religion. Actually, however, they were ordinarily more accessible to the high castes with a tradition of learning, employment in the government and urban residence.

In the Indian context the studies of social mobility have mainly been carried out in terms of departures from traditional caste–based occupations. In 1954, a survey of Poona indicated that the traditional relationship between caste and occupation had considerably changed. Thus, Brahmins are found in all occupations except in unskilled, manual work (Ghurye, 1969).

In an industrial society, one's achievement and also life style form important criteria. Income and education play an important role, but not one's caste. Thus, industrialists, doctors, lawyers, professors and other highly educated people as well as those who have achieved importance in their special field, constitute largely the upper status groups. The criteria used to mark them out are wealth, progressive views, good education, refinement or social service and achievement in their respective field (Pande, 1986).

According to D' Souza's study (1985), it is a well-known fact that the traditional society in India was stratified into castes. The different caste groups practiced different types of occupations. The status hierarchy of the caste groups corresponded with the prestige hierarchy of occupations followed by their members. The findings of this study show that the caste system, which is an important aspect of the social structure of the communities, modifies the influence of economic development. By and large, the fruits of economic development have gone to the members of different castes according to the position of their castes in the caste hierarchy. The higher castes have benefitted more than lower ones. Even among the higher castes themselves, some castes have benefitted from the new opportunities more than others. Thus, the new economic opportunities have been channelled through the caste system. The new opportunities have affected the trade and service sectors the most. The castes which have benefitted most from these opportunities are the traditional trading castes of Banias and Khatris and the professional castes, such as the Brahmins.

Social inequality is a key note of the caste system. In this system there is superiority of one caste over the other. It is more accurate to think of the caste system as constituting a multiplicity of hierarchies determined by custom with in various geographical area of organisation. The relationship of one caste to another is not similar to that which exists between master and slave. The inferior-superior relationship of a caste may be stated in terms of its purity. In this context, Ketkar remarks: "A caste is pure or impure according to its hierarchical position" (Ketkar, 1909). Untouchability is the characteristic fact of Hindu society. The caste system constitutes the structure of Hinduism as a religion is a system beliefs and doctrines developed about the basic principle of Karma. Caste is the very core of Hindu religion. As M.K. Gandhi observe: "If untouchability was a part of the Hindu creed. I should decline to call myself a Hindu and most decidedly embrace some other faith if it is satisfied my honest aspirations." Gandhi further states, "Fortunately for me, I hold that untouchability is not a part of Hinduism" (Gandhi, 1927). Caste is such an obtrusive factor of Indian social organisation. During the British rule the untouchables were really unapproachable. Gandhi says, "Untouchability means pollution by the touch of certain persons by reason of their birth in a particular state of family" (Hingorani, 1961). Caste system generates the feeling of 'superiority' or 'inferiority' in minds of caste-based society. Untouchability is described as a sin, blot, curse and stain imposed on a group of people by another group of people.

Mulk Raj Anand's novel *The Big Heart* (1945) describe in the context of caste conflict in India and focuses on the significant theme of untouchability. To begin with, the story exposes the conflict between sub-castes. Thathiars and Kasera are the sub-castes in the community of the copper-smiths. Ananta, the protagonist is a coppersmith, who belongs to the Thathiars and returns to his home in the Billimaran Kucha of Amritsar. After having worked in factories in Bombay and Ahmedabad, he brings his beloved Janki, a young widow, with him. In this Town, Lala Murli Dhar and Seth Gokul Chand have established a factory which manufactures war tools. It has created a peculiar unrest. Many Thathiars have been rendered jobless because of the introduction of the machine. Ananta tries together all, the jobless coppersmiths into a union. So, they can demand their jobs and justice from the factory owner, the capitalists.

The caste and class conflicts are finely interrelated to each other in the novel. Anand exposes the interpersonal relations among the high castes. Kasera and Thathiar are sub-castes of the Kshatriya coppersmith community. Kaseras suppose themselves superior to the Thathiars and they would be polluted by contact with the sub-caste. They believe in a legend. "To Ram was given an arrow, to Sita bow, and from them the truly Nobel order of Kshatriya Kaseras is descended" (Anand, 1945, 129). This deep-rooted caste consciousness is revealed by Mulk Raj Anand. The Big Heart touches on both caste and class problems, showing how they react on each other! The Thathiars endlessly suffer at the hands of the rich Kaseras. Ananta is conscious of it, as he says; "…. We suffer from the day we born till the day we die, but this cruelty is unnecessary. A little reason could settle this difficulty between the Kaseras and us" (Anand, 1945, 136). He has described the two groups of these two sub-castes in the following words: '….the beautiful copper, brass, silver and bronze utensils made in the lane are sold by dealers called Kaseras; …..' In the new Iron Monger's bazaar…..these are thc screws, bolts, nails and locks are sold by Thathiars….." The Thathiars are lower because they work with their hands. As Anand points out: "……..the Thathiars are craftsman, doing dirty, grimy, ill-paid work, with their hands had come to acquire a low professional status in Hindu society" (Anand, 1945, 127).

Gokul Chand is a kasera and the choudhari of utensil seller's community. Lala Murli Dhar is a thathiar and the leading person in the coppersmith brotherhood. They established a factory manufacturing war tools. Their relations are based on cash nexus. They are partners, but their friendship seems to be stained because of caste differences. Anand has tried to project the interaction of the two evil – class and caste in the Big Heart. As M.K. Naik observe: "In Billimaran– the worst in old tradition joins hand with the worst in modern capitalism in an unholy alliance of forces of exploitation". The caste and class conflict in the novel is not as dominant as in Anand's earlier novels. But the Big Heart dwells on an aspect of casteism that has not received any serious attention (Prasad, 2001).

In this chapter an attempt has been made to know about changes in the caste system of Thathiars, emergence of economic inequalities within the caste, caste changing into class. Beside this, their interpersonal and inter-caste relations and their representation in religious spheres have been analysed.

Changes in the Caste System

The concept of hierarchy is one of the most essential features of the caste system. To know about the hierarchical status of castes in Jandiala Guru, information has been collected about the different caste groups of the town. These caste groups are Brahmin, Khatri, Arora, Jain, Jat, Kamboj, Suniare, Tank-Kshatriya, Ramgarhia, Mehra and Sudra. It is important to know that out of these castes, which caste is at the top of hierarchy in town. The information was collected from the respondents. Thirty five per cent respondents mentioned that the Brahmins are at the top of hierarchy, while another 28 per cent think Khatris, 17 per cent mentioned Aroras and 20 per cent thought Jats to be at the top of hierarchy.

Sudras are at the bottom of the hierarchy while 66 per cent respondents mentioned and 34 per cent believe that both Mehras and Sudras are at the bottom of hierarchy.

Information regarding dominant castes in the town reveals that 37 per cent respondents mentioned Brahmin and Khatri castes are the dominant castes. Other 24 per cent think Khatri and Arora castes have dominant hold in the town, while 28 per cent replied that the Khatri caste is the dominant caste. Only 11 per cent consider that the Brahmin caste is the dominant caste in the Jandiala Guru town.

Reasons for this dominance are multiple. Table 4.1 shows that 31.78 per cent think dominance in occupation is the main cause of dominant caste, because this shows command or hold of that caste (dominant caste) person over the economic zone. That's why a large proportion of the population of the town works with them. Other 27.81 per cent think this happens according to hierarchical placement which is in our society, i.e., Brahmin, Khatri, Vaishya, and Sudra. Another 25.89 per cent think due to numerical preponderance, which caste population is more in numbers than other caste group. Only 14.52 per cent are those who think that financial position plays an important role in the status of caste.

Table 4.1
Reasons for Dominance of Caste

Reasons	*Number*	*Percentage*
Dominance in occupation	151	31.78
Hierarchical placement	132	27.81
Numerically preponderant	123	25.89
Financially strong	69	14.52
Total	**475***	**100.00**

* Multiple Responses

To know about respondents own caste placement in the hierarchy, question asked to them was, where would you place your own caste in the caste hierarchy? In this regard, response of 21 per cent respondents is that they place their own caste at the top. Another 39 per cent place it at the middle and 40 per cent place it at the bottom in the caste hierarchy.

Regarding high or low status of caste groups, the respondents believe that our society is caste-based society. Division of castes creates inequality. A large proportion that is, 68 per cent respondents informed that they believe in high or low status of caste. Other 32 per cent said we do not believe in the status of caste. Table 4.2 reveals the various reasons for believing in the status of caste. Proportion of 38.40 per cent respondents said that the society has created inequality among human beings which is prevailing from the traditional times. Reply of 27.34 per cent respondents is because of caste status that a person belongs to upper, middle or lower caste. Another 23.88 per cent think caste has always prevailed in our personal and social lives, especially at the time of marriage. Other 10.38 per cent said caste system governs all aspects of our lives.

Table 4.2
Reasons for believing in Status of Caste

Reasons	*Number*	*Percentage*
Society created difference	111	38.40
Because of the caste status	79	27.34
Caste always prevail in our lives	69	23.88
Its governs our life	30	10.38
Total	**289***	**100.00**

* Multiple Responses

On the other hand, 32 per cent are those who don't believe in caste status. Table 4.3 reveals the reasons for not doing so. 47.66 per cent mentioned that there is nothing in the system of caste. What is caste? It has no meaning in life. Only we human beings create such differences, which

Table 4.3
Reasons for not believing in Caste Status

Reasons	*Number*	*Percentage*
Nothing is in this caste system	71	47.66
All are equal	49	32.88
God is the Creator of everything	29	19.46
Total	**149***	**100.00**

* Multiple Responses

are harmful for society. Other 32.88 per cent realised that all are equal. There should be no discrimination on the basis of caste while 19.46 per cent said God is the Creator of everything or every person.

To know about the changes in the caste position another question relating to the changes was asked from the respondents: Do you think people can change their caste position? Regarding this, 37 per cent mentioned that people can change their caste position and 63 per cent said people cannot change their caste position. Fifty four per cent respondents, who believe that change in caste is possible, mentioned that financial position of the person is the way to change caste position in today's life. While, forty six per cent think that through intercaste marriage, caste position can be changed. If a person of lower caste marries to a person of higher caste, this may bring change in the caste position. Another sixty three per cent, who think, caste position cannot be changed, they said it is a God's gift. We got it by birth, we can't change it.

Without reference to caste or the social identities that influenced economic mobility deeply in the contemporary crafts, manifestly in textiles and leather. Among weavers, who were divided in a complex and elaborate hierarchy, social status often indicated entrepreneurial prospects, being associated with the product woven, with ability and willingness to acquire technical and general learning, and with business institutions involving some form of informal cooperations. With tanners, their degraded status in the village was clearly a major factor in the urbanisation of the industry, emigration of labour, and creation of labour markets out of a customary transaction, as hides acquired a market outside the village.

The number and population of brass-ware castes were smaller than in textiles, and socially brass-workers were not underprivileged in the way leather artisans were. In northern

India, stretching the region southward to include Deccan, the three main castes were the Kasera or Kasar or Kansari, the Thathera or Thathiar, and the Tamera or Tambat. They were unevenly distributed, with Kasera concentration increasing towards the east, Thatheras towards the north, and Tambats in central India. The Thatheras included a large number of Muslims. Etymologically, the first could be identified with brass or bronze, the third with copper, and from the way the name sounds, the Thatheras were likely to have been wielders of the hammer. The Tameras, indeed, were a small and probably depleting group in the early twentieth century, reflecting the fate of pure copper work. The other two were said to be as freely taking up other occupations as outsiders were entering brass, but the census statistics on caste-work correspondence, the usual means to infer such changes, are not detailed enough to confirm this. The metal-wise and process-wise specialisations, if any, between them had also long since disappeared.

The comparative homogeneity of the work, and of the workers, may account for the following two features of the industry. First, it may explain why, unlike in cloth, social inequalities did not show up in striking ways in brass. And relatedly, the distance between the merchants and the artisans was much less sharp than in crafts like textiles or leather. The two 'classes' in brass-ware were usually from the same caste, or at least, classes did not indicate systematic social origins. If this impression holds, it would define brass as an industry with prospects of economic mobility relatively unhampered by features of the artisan society.

Recognising that merchants and workers were not socially divided makes it easier to tackle the rather confusing attempts at defining caste occupations in the twentieth-century sources. According to N. M. Joshi, Poona Kasars were master-hammerers in the 1880s; the Nasik ones were rich dealers. L. C. Jain's evidence before the United Provinces

Banking Enquiry suggests that the Moradabad merchants were Hindu banias (Kaseras?), whereas the workers were Muslims many north Indian Thatheras were Muslims). Chaturvedi's Moradabad survey twenty years later, however, shows that merchants too were predominantly Muslims. P. G. Shah's informative article at the Bankipore industrial conference of 1912 identified Kasars as the 'capitalist class', and Thatheras as the 'workmen class'. In Bengal, Kansari is a corrupt of Kansabanik, 'banik' standing for merchant. If these usages seem temptingly suggestive of a pattern, Denzil Ibbetson frustrates it by confidently asserting that 'the Thathera is the man who sells, as the Kasera is the man who makes vessels'. And Enthoven's equally eminent caste anthology of 1922 describes an origin-myth of the Gujarat Kaseras unambiguously defining them as hammerers (c.f. Roy, 1996).

It is indeed plausible that the man who became a merchant was usually engaged in cast-metal work, that is, possessing enough resources to maintain a furnace, crucibles and adequate space, and able to turn out articles that could add value by polishing, plating or engraving. It is also plausible that the hammerer, whose job was basically physical labour intensive, was usually the person without capital. Further, but here we are rather speculative, in their origins; the Kaseras might have been the cast-metal workers and Thatheras the hammerers (Roy, 1996).

The present study which is about the Thathiars of Jandiala Guru, show some changes in the status of the Thathiar caste. Thathiar, which is an artisan caste, handles the metals and make utensils manually. They work in brass, copper, bronze and other metals with the exception of iron and tin. As they were working with their hands and the nature of their work was such, they were placed low in the caste ranking. But mythically they claimed to have a status of Khatri caste. But as a result of the Green Revolution and its consequences on the lives of the people on the one hand and the penetration of machine made utensils of metal, plastic, porcelains etc. in the urban and rural market, on the other, transformed the lives of the traditional Thathiars. The respondents have also narrated that in the 1950s the poor working and living conditions led them to approach Partap Singh Kairon, the Chief Minister of Punjab, asking for a backward caste status, which entitled them to quota for raw material, expensive metals, reservation in government jobs, and scholarship for study of children. Therefore, for all purposes of enumeration the Thathiars were taken as backward caste. In common list of OBCs state Punjab on December 7, 2011 Thathiars are registered on 46th ranks their caste or community names enlisted as Thathora and Tampora (realinfo.tv/index.php?topic=8110.0). As the benefits of the Green Revolution were percolated to all sections of the society, the Thathiars also experienced the possibilities of diversifications in their traditional work. They introduced changes in their work. Some of them started manufacturing units; some took to contractual work, others to the sale of the utensils. Many of the traditional Thathiars joined these factories as skilled workers. The change in their work made them economically better off than before. This change in occupation brought change in caste status. Hence they started claiming a Khatri caste status. The Khatri occupies a very different position among the people of the Punjab from Banyas, Dhunsars, Pahari Mahajan, Suds and Bhabars. Superior to them in physique, in manliness and in energy, he is not, like them, a mere shopkeeper. He claims, indeed, to be a direct representative of the Kshatriya of Manu, but the validity of the claim is as doubtful as other matters connected with the fourfold caste system. Trade is their main occupation, but in fact they have broader and more distinguishing features (Ibbetson, 1974).

The introduction of other material like steel glass, plastic, porcelain etc. in the utensil making has changed the taste of the people. This ultimately led to the reduction in the demand of metal products. On the other hand younger generation shows no interest in this work. They think that this work carries lower status. The work is noisy and physically tough comparative to other kinds of work. They have started taking to other jobs/ occupations rather than utensil making. Due to change in their occupation, they consider themselves as Khatri by caste (which is high, trading caste). The reason they give is that now they are not in the occupation of the Thathiar caste which was backward. Therefore, they ceased to be Thathiars. By virtue of taking to other trading occupations, they have started claiming the status of Khatri caste. The pattern of their mobility is associated with the changed nature of the occupation.

Emergence of Economic Inequalities within the Caste

The existence of unequal opportunities and reward for different social positions or status with a group or society creates inequalities. Here the purpose is to discuss the emergence of economic inequalities within the caste in the context of their representation in social, political and religious spheres and interpersonal and inter-caste relations.

Representation in Social and Political Sphere

To know about the representation in social and political spheres, the information has been collected from the respondents about customs/ practices of caste, marriage, and social relations of caste and about caste association. In this regard, 10 per cent respondents informed that the customs/ practices of their caste are different from other castes in any way. Thirty nine per cent respondents argue that there is no difference. Other 51 per cent think that some of the customs/ practices are different. These distinctive customs relate to birth, marriage and death ceremonies. A custom of 'Reetaa' performed in the seventh month of pregnancy. Parents of the lady bring white dupatta and some other things for her and family. Another ritual related to marriage which is strictly performed by this caste person is to take bath in the holy water of Ganges before one week of the marriage. They believe that this performance would make them pure for new life. All these acts are the great facts of life, which move within the framework of caste.

About marriage related decisions, all the respondents replied that they marry within their own caste. Rather they would select the mate out of the sub-castes of their own caste, i.e., Verma, Suri, Anand, Malhotra, Kaushalaya, and Dhobi etc. But they do not select mate out of all the sub-castes of the caste. Because, same sub-caste persons are perceive as brother-sister. There is no way to establish marriage relations among them.

In the Thathiar community of the town, only twelve cases of inter-caste and inter-religious marriage could be found. Among these, four cases are of inter-caste marriage and eight cases are of inter-religious marriage. Five inter-religious marriages have been performed between the Hindus and Sikhs, two between Jains and Hindus and one between Muslims and Sikhs. On the other hand, two inter-caste marriages took place of Ramgarhias, one with Arora's and one with Mehra caste group.

While giving information about social relations with these caste people, 62 per cent mentioned that they have social relations only with high and middle caste people, i.e., Arora, Jat, Kamboj, Ramgarhia, Tank-Kashatriya etc. and not with lower castes. While 29 per cent of respondents said they have social relations only with those caste groups who are in their neighbourhoods, only 19 per cent are those who said they have no social relations with other caste people. Because their place of work and residence are at different places. That's why they have social relations only with their own caste people. Those who have relations, they said, we invite them to attend birth, marriage and death ceremonies. Sometimes we attend their ceremonies if they invite us. We participate in each other's family functions.

Caste Association

Association is a formal group organised for a specialised and specifically stated purpose by a specific caste group. An association has established rules of organisation and procedure, or formalised system of leadership and certain common interests among its members. Because of the limited involvement of the members, impersonal or secondary relations predominate (Sharma, 1992).

About the information of caste association, 76 per cent mentioned that they have caste association. Other 24 per cent said they have no caste association, while 49 per cent are the members of this association. The name of this association is "Thathiar Association". This association has 100 to 150 members. Mostly those persons have strong hold in the caste association whose occupational standing is good and who are financially sound. Association has one president, one vice-president, one secretary and one cashier. After two or three months they gather at Singh Sabha Gurdwara, Kashmirian Bazaar, for meeting where they discuss various issues like planning for how to celebrate the religious functions, i.e., Gurpurab, Shivratri, Jagran etc. Besides this, they discuss problems related to occupation and social and personal aspects. Occupational problems are regarding wages, supply of raw material, marketing etc. They discuss all these issues in association meetings and try to resolve it. From social point of view if the members of the caste have any conflict with other caste members, any religious conflicts etc. are the major concern. If any member of the association has any serious personal problem regarding family, they show concern for help.

But on the other hand, those who are not satisfied with the association work and who are not the members of this association said that association has nothing to do. It creates unnecessary conflicts between the members and others.

Every caste group in the town has caste association. These are Arora, Ramgarhia, Jain, Mehra associations.

Most of the respondents replied that they do not know about the number of members in these caste associations. "Our caste association plays role to solve our problems in the same way every caste association plays role for the benefits of its own caste". Sometimes these associations perform mutual functions, falling in the social sphere or inter-caste issues like inter-caste marriages, inter-religious disputes etc. In these circumstances these association play significant role.

Representation in Religious Spheres

Religion is a system of belief, practices and philosophical values concerned with the definition of the sacred, the comprehension of life and salvation from the problems of human existence (Sharma, 1992).

Religion has great influence upon the life. Every caste has religious place to worship. From this aspect, 82 per cent said, to worship they have religious place of caste. Other 18 per cent think every religious place is a place of worship for them. Religious places of caste are Bhadarkali Mandir, which is situated outside of the Shekhfatha Gate, presently managed by Udasi-saint, Jatena Gurudwara and Singh Sabha Gurdwara. Both the latter places were established by the Thathiar community. Sikh Thathiars have great devotion for these places.

Regarding respondents' information about to whom they worship, 22.44 per cent replied that they worship Bhadarkali Mandir. Other 21.56 per cent worship Gurdwara Baba Hundal, who was the founder of this town (Jandiala Guru).

Baba Hundal was born in a Jat family. His father's name was 'Ghazi', who performed services of Majawar on a Pir's grave. His mother's name was 'Mai Sukhi'. According to a legend, Baba Hundal while grazing cattle used to get spiritual lessons from a Nath Jogi, at the place near the present gurdwara. On sudden disappearance of the Jogi, Baba felt depressed and went to the Golden Temple. There he started meditating on the banks of the sarovar (holy tank). On being approached by the relatives of Baba Hundal, Guru Arjan Dev asked Hundal to return home. Baba made a promise to the guru that he will return home after completion of his meditation of 12 years. At the end of his meditation, Baba Hundal met his preceptor and returned to Jandiala, where he demolished the grave of Pir, where his father worked as Majawar. On his so doing the local Muslim residents started beating the Baba. At this juncture it so happened that the houses of the Muslims caught fire. The more they tried to extinguish the fire, the fiercer it became. Ultimately, the Muslims sought forgiveness of the Baba and fire subsided. Baba Hundal founded the sect of Niranjania who believe in Adi-Granth and the ten Sikh built at the place, where Baba Hundal received lessons, now called Nathan Da Dhera, presently managed by an Udasi-saint. Fairs are held every year on 28-29 Baisakh (April) and on 1st Magh (January) according to the Bikrami Calendar (Census, 1991). This community has great devotion for this place.

Dhera Dhyanpur which is situated in Dhyanpur village of Gurdaspur district was established by Baba Lal ji. 21.37 per cent members of this community go to this place. Another 34.63 per cent worship Singh Sabha and Jateana Gurdwara.

Information collected from the respondents reveal that 64 per cent said the members of other castes and communities come to attend the religious functions. These communities are Hindu, Sikh and Jain. Caste groups are Jat, Arora, Suniare, Tank-Kashatriya, Ramgarhia and Mehra. Jain community has occupational relations with the Thathiar community. Very few members of this community have close relations with Thathiar caste persons, who come to attend only their religious functions. Most of the members of other caste groups which are mentioned above have neighbourhood relations. A very small proportion is of those who have close family social relations with this caste group.

Interpersonal and Intercaste Relations

In the case of their interpersonal and inter-caste relations most of their family and personal friends are of the same caste. Some are from Arora, Tank-Kshatriya, Mehra and Ramgarhia castes. Their same caste friends are involved mainly in utensil making and some are in other occupations. Friends of other castes are engaged in business like that of general store, grocery, electronic goods, accountancy and skilled work of carpentary etc.

Regarding inter-relationship, 83 per cent mentioned that their caste has some restrictions upon them. These restrictions are mainly about marriage related decisions. Our caste does not permit us to marry with other caste groups, they said. But they have inter-dining relations only with those persons with whom, they have family relations and neighbourhood relations. They have inter-dining with Ramgarhias, Tank-Kashatriyas, Aroras and Mehras. While 17 per cent are those who said that they have no restrictions upon them by their caste. They mentioned they have inter-relationship with other caste group except Sudras.

Reaction of Other Caste Group

When different caste groups deal with each other, there is usual reaction among the members of different caste groups. On being interviewed, 74 per cent said that other caste groups whenever invited by us happily visit the occasions. Because they invite only those people with whom they have relations. It may be family, social and neighbourhood relations. On the other hand 26 per cent said that the members of Jain and Brahmin communities unwillingly visit the occasion. It is because with Jain community they have only occupational or economic relations and Brahmins feel themselves superior to other castes. They hesitate to come on any occasion of happiness or sorrow.

In sum, here we can say that there are changes in the caste system of the Thathiars. The Thathiars, who were traditional artisans, got themselves registered as backward caste. But now they have become Khatris. This change in caste is due to change in occupation. Those who have moved from traditional Thathiar work and joined other jobs/ occupations in utensil-making, they call themselves Khatri by caste. In the social sphere, their custom and practices are different in few manners than other caste groups. They have social relationship with Arora, Ramgarhia, Jat, Kamboj, Tank-Kshatriya castes. Caste association plays an important role within the caste group and with other caste groups. Thathiars have their own places of worship. Only those members of other castes and communities come to attend religious function to which they invite. Most of their personal and family friends are of their own caste. But they have inter-relation with high and middle castes. Those persons of other castes, with whom Thathiar community have relations happily visit the occasion whenever invited by them. But the Jain and Brahmin community keep reservations about participating in their functions.

5

Work Processes

In the previous chapter discussion centred on the changes in the caste system of the Thathiars, which took place due to changes in the occupational structure. With the advent of industrialisation traditional Thathiars are moving towards other jobs or occupations than utensil making. With the change in occupation, they have changed their caste status. Due to poor working and living conditions they claimed for backward caste status. But, now with the change in occupation they consider themselves as Khatri by caste. Besides this, their interpersonal, intercaste relations and their representation in religious spheres have been discussed.

The present chapter examines the changing character of various processes of the work of the Thathiars. Some significant issues viz. skill formation, organisation of work, participation of the family, difficulties in setting up, raw material and the main products of the Thathiars will be given considerable attention. The focus is on the changes which have taken place in the occupation due to the technological development.

Originally craftwork tended to be concentrated in the towns and craftsmen made up a relatively small proportion of the population. They were usually organised in guilds, adhering to a strict apprentice system and to other rules covering the way their trade was to be carried out. The guild fixed rules of work and the quality of the finished product and its price to safeguard both the artisan and the customer. The guild also controlled the prices of manufactured articles and they depended on the quality of the work or were calculated according to a fixed scale. The behaviour of guild members was controlled through guild court (Thapar, 1968). The basic crafts were textiles, clothing, leather, metal-working and the processing of food and drink. These provided employment for roughly three quarters of the urban population. Unlike today, particular industries were not necessarily concentrated in one part of the country though this was occasionally made necessary as in metal-working, for example, by the need for access to raw material. However, poor communication meant that access to markets was a strong influence on industrial location; industries were largely situated where there were customers (Gadgil, 1972).

It is the technological change which contributes a lot to the changes in social relationship. The industrial technology, particularly division of labour and mechanisation has certain important consequences for the worker's role. Not only does industrial technology determine what the worker does, his functions for the plant, but it determines the conditions under which he will perform his functions. The results of industrial technology on the worker's role are diversification, specialisation, reduction of skills, reutilisation, the reduction of the importance of the role, isolation and the creation of special physical condition. In general, division of labour helped in various ways to determine the social relations at work. Specialisation, for instance, helped to create the specific roles which individual played within the factory. The division of labour also plays a part in creating certain strains in the social relations at work (Schneider, 1957).

Technological development gives rise to differentiation of functions. Smelser (1963) points out that development leads to a differentiation of functions in the society. Work once performed by a single social unit, i.e., occupational and other activities becomes separated from their traditional basis. Changing the methods and tools with which work is done inevitably results into social change. This includes relations among workers, family members and between the sexes vis-à-vis work. Moreover, new work places find a worker in a different relationship with regard to his own life cycle.

Schneider (1957) has commented that machine has fundamentally reversed the nature of the relationship between man and his instrument of production. The tool is merely the extension of the man's hand. The hammer obeys the impulses of the worker, operates due to the energy supplied by him, and responds to his thoughts, habits, skills; whereas the worker in modern industry is exactly having the opposite relation to the machine. It is the machine which determines the worker's action, the energies he will expend, and the skills he can employ. The power is supplied from a distant source. The speed of the process is controlled automatically and needed skills are reduced to elementary movements. In some cases the worker who performs a particular job, is ignorant of its place in the whole system of production. Consequently, he may experience a lack of interest in his job, a sense of meaninglessness and purposelessness in existence which are responsible for a variety of strains in the worker's role resulting in reduced skilled performance.

Skill Formation

In all differentiated societies, the emergence of specialised occupational skills, whether produce of goods or services create relationship of social and economic dependence and paradoxically relationship of social distance (Johnson, 1972). The process of skill formation undergoes some transformation due to shift from tools to machine technology. Modernisation of work influences traditional skills. Some of the skills are becoming obsolete while some are still relevant to operate the machines. Thus, the growth of service industries, specialist skills, aerospace industries and automation has all contributed to the decline in the proportion of unskilled or semi-skilled worker (Schneider, 1957). Here, some sources of skill formation, i.e., age at learning the skill, motivating factors to learn the skills, sources of learning the skill will be discussed.

Motivating Factors to take up the Occupation

It is expected that a person who has acquired a skill would take it up as an economic activity. Data reveal in Table 5.1 that a good number of respondents, i.e., 22.37 per cent have taken this occupation because it was their hereditary occupation. They learn skill from their fathers and grand-fathers, who gave them experience and training. Other 21.63 per cent were motivated because of good market and profitable business. Economic necessity and earning also motivate respondents to take up this occupation for

Table 5.1
Motivating Factors to Learn the Skill

Factors	*Number*	*Percentage*
Hereditary occupation	123	22.37
Good market/Profitable business	119	21.63
Economic necessity	96	17.46
For earning/Livelihood	81	14.72
Because of interest	72	13.10
Friends/Relatives are in business	59	10.72
Total	**550***	**100.00**

*Multiple Responses

living. Some joined because of their personal interest in this work. Only 10.72 per cent took up this occupation because their friends and relatives were in this occupation.

Utensil making is skillful occupation. Every person engaged in this work has learnt the skill from direct or indirect sources. Table 5.2 shows that a large proportion of Thathiars have learnt the skill from private apprenticeship. Private apprentices include all those who have learnt the skill from grand-father, father, brother or any other relative or any other trained person. In this process traditional Thathiar or any experienced person is recognised as guru by the person who wants to learn the skill. After learning, he offers rupee eleven and raw-sugar (*gur*) to the guru. Those workers whose grandfathers and fathers were in this work from the beginning, they share the real work and real problems. They learn the trade secrets and learn the forms and theory of his branch of the tradition. A large proportion 65.34 per cent of workers learnt the skill through private apprenticeship. This makes them perfect in their work. They complete their training over a period of two months to six months. They develop full expertise about a single product or unit, which the workers choose. Generally, the apprentice is paid rupees 15 to 20 a week. Those workers who are from other castes, utensil making was not their hereditary occupation; they faced problems in learning the skill. The traditional Thathiars do not want to share the secrets of the work with any outcaste person.

Another factor in Table 5.2 shows age at which Thathiars learn the skill. It starts at quiet early age and has gone upto 30 years of age. The reason for this is that the hereditary Thathiars usually learn the skill through apprenticeship which starts from the childhood in his house itself. Other 21.66 per cent learnt on the job and 13 per cent learnt through experience and observation, their percentage is less than those who learnt through the apprenticeship. They start it at the age of fifteen. After practice, they

Table 5.2

Sources and Age at Learning the Skill

Age (in years)	*Sources*			*Total*
	Private apprenticeship	*On the job*	*Learnt through experience*	
Up to 10	12	00	00	12 (4.00)
11-14	23	00	00	23 (07.66)
15-18	49	12	08	69 (23.00)
19-22	82	16	09	107 (35.67)
23-26	07	23	18	48 (16.00)
27-30	15	13	02	30 (10.00)
After 30	08	01	02	11 (03.67)
Total	**196 (65.34)**	**65 (21.66)**	**39 (13.00)**	**300 (100.00)**

Figures within parenthesis indicate percentages.

start independently, which delays their entrance into the occupation.

Nature of Work

With the passage of time, nature of work undergoes changes, which have taken place due to industrialisation, modernisation, awareness and in the present times due to globalisation.

Industrialisation brings about great changes in the work technology. The ways of doing work in traditional times, have changed in the present times. Traditional workers performed their work with hand tools. Now their work has shifted from hand tools to machines.

The basic conflict in The Big Heart is between the forces of tradition and modernity, and this is evident in the setting of novel-Billimaran or the Cat-Killer's Lane:

It must be remembered, however, that Billimaran is not a blind alley. A part from the usual mouth, which even a cul de sac keeps open, it has another, which makes it really like a two-headed snake. With one head it looks towards the ancient market, where the beautiful copper, brass, silver and bronze utensils made in the lane are sold by dealers called Kaseras, hence called Bazar Kaserian. With the other it wriggles out towards the new Ironmongers' Bazar, where screws, bolts, nails and locks are sold and which merge into the Bookseller's mart, the cigarette shops and the post office with the spirit of modern times.

The Ironmonger's Bazar stands for the machine, and thus modernity, while the Bazar Kaserian stands for tradition. The fettering images by which modernity is symbolised—'screws, bolts, nails and locks'– show the author's ingrained partiality against tradition. But time has wrought a change, and time is moving with every measured stroke of the 'gigantic four-faced English clock,' which vies for attention with the shrine of the Goddess

Kali in the shabby lane. The temple and the clock also represent tradition and modernity respectively. And though the author and his spokesmen Ananta and the poet see the evils of the machine age and the benefits of the old way of life, they realise that the older order is obsolete in a country on the verge of a vast social, economic and political change (Anand, 1945).

The nature of the Thathiars' work, i.e., utensil making, in the past was in the hands of traditional Thathiars, *dalals* or contractors and shopkeepers. The traditional Thathiars were mainly dependent upon government for raw material; however, they would also procure scrap from local dealers/ shopkeepers. The whole process of work was manual. These traditional Thathiars made the products and sold it to shopkeepers, contractors and sometimes directly to the customers. A few were performing the role of *dalal* or contractor.

Industrialisation introduces machines in the work process, which diversified the work; this gave rise to manufacturers, wholesalers, retailers, contractors and skilled workers. Along with this, modernisation and awareness among workers moulded them towards new work processes, which introduced new combinations of work activities, i.e., manufacturer-cum-contractor, contractor-cum-shopkeepers etc. In the present time of globalisation, individual's interest in traditional work has changed due to varieties of other occupations being available.

Thus in this process, the traditional Thathiars, were the backbone of the utensil making. In the traditional times, they depended upon government for raw material. In the present time, they purchase raw material from local market. Their process of work has been changed. They are using their traditional tools, along with the use of modern machines. Those who are manufacturers, have their own independent processing unit, i.e., small-scale workshops and factories. They supervise the whole production process. Purchasing of raw material, maintaining quality of the products and supervision of workers are under their control. They purchase the raw material from local shopkeepers and they fix the wages of the skilled workers. On the other hand, manufacturers are engaged in the job of manufacturing as well as contracting. They arrange contracts with skilled worker, traditional Thathiars and shopkeepers for fixed period. They deal with workers for manufacturing or shaping the utensils and with shopkeepers to sell the products. The contract may be for ten days to one month, not more than this. Shopkeepers purchase ready material from manufacturers, contractors and from traditional Thathiars. Among the respondents some are wholesalers and some are retailers. Sometimes these sellers purchase from out of the town or state for variety of the products. In traditional times, traditional Thathiars sold directly to the customers. Some shops are of raw/waste material. Another occupation is of contractor-cum-shopkeepers, in this they get ready material from the workers or from factories with a fixed contract, on commission basis. According to weight, they fix the commission. It is two per cent of 10 kg/weight. After this, they sell the products directly to the local market within the state or outside the state. The contractor or *dalal* mainly works with traditional Thathiars and skilled workers on the contract basis. They fix the wages according to the days, i.e., Rs 80 per day. With the mechanisation of traditional work, many people got displaced from work. Some of them later became skilled workers in the factories. They had traditional skills in the work. Due to financial problems, they are not able to purchase developed or modern machines for work. That is why, they work with the manufacturer and contractor and known as skilled workers.

Table 5.3 shows that in the period from 1911 to 1920 there were eight traditional Thathiars and two retail shopkeepers (Kaseras) in the town. From 1921 to 1930, there were six

Thathiars and two retail shopkeepers. Between 1931 and 1940, traditional Thathiars were eight, who made products by using traditional techniques, three were contractors-cum-shopkeepers who had their shops of utensil selling, five were contractors and two were running shops of utensils.

From 1941 to 1950, when industrialisation had started taking place in work process, three units of manufacturing got established, where the work was performed with modern techniques. Seven persons had joined these manufacturing units as skilled workers. From 1951 to 1960, manufacturers were three, contractor-cum-shopkeepers were seven and skilled workers were twenty five. In the period from 1961 to 1980 the number of skilled workers was highest.

The table further shows that at present traditional Thathiars are 80 (26.66 per cent). Total manufacturers are 17 (5.66 per cent), manufacturers-cum-contractors are 16 (5.34 per cent), wholesalers are 3 per cent, retailers are 8.66 per cent and shops of utensils raw/waste materials (*kachha mal*) are 1.34 per cent. A large proportion which is 97, i.e., 32.34 per cent has become skilled workers in the factories. Table also reveals that a large proportion of persons joined the occupation during the two time phases of 1941-60 and 1961-80. In the first phase due to Indo-Pak partition, a large proportion migrated to this place which was the main market for utensil making and people also took up this occupation due to the availability of work. In the second phase, it was due to the prosperity of the people as an outcome of the Green Revolution and with the advent of industrialisation. In 1947, when partition took place, 31.87 per cent migrated from Pakistan. Out of these 13.87 per cent were those whose hereditary occupation was utensil making. Other 18 per cent joined due to availability of this work. Before migration they were in the occupation of general merchants, *karyana* shopkeepers and factory workers.

Activities Performed in the Production Process

Most locations of brass-wares in the early twentieth century were characterised by a three-tier exchange of products and labour, the 'classes' engaged being termed dealers, *karkhanadars*, and workers. Chatterjee's description in 1907 of the usual practice in United Provinces had the dealer obtaining scrap from the peddlers, and the 'head-man' of a brass factory turning it into wares for a charge (c.f. Roy, 1996). Between one place and another, the dealer could be more or less specialised, and more or less distinct from the *karkhanadars*. Similarly, systems of work and payments at the shop-floor could differ as well. But in general, work was bound almost everywhere by a contract between a merchant and a sort of headman of the workers. Contrary to impressions, '*karkhanadar*' might or might not be an actual workshop-owner, but he was invariably a worker-intermediary, and an employer of labour.

The uniformity with which the three-tier exchange, and the Karkhanas or workshop, appear in early descriptions of brass-wares derives to some extent from a technological reason. Before the imports of brass sheets, and in cast-metal work even after imports started, the main capital needed in the work was a furnace which required, at a time, three to five workers to operate and fully utilise. The entire requirement of labour could not come from the family, since female labour was not usually employed in metals. A well-developed apprenticeship helped recruit unpaid assistants, often from within the family. But the craft still required non-family labour, to a much greater extent than, say, textiles (Roy, 1996).

In the process of production, different types of activities are performed by workers. Table 5.4 shows that 26.66 per cent respondents are performing traditional Thathiar work. Other 32.34 per cent are skilled workers. They work in other's small-scale workshops and factories. The work of traditional Thathiars is manual. They work for long hours in a day. They beat the metal to turn into vessels. Sellers of utensils are 11.66 per cent, they get ready material from traditional Thathiars, manufacturers and contractors and sometimes from out of the state for variety which includes various types of utensils like pots, pans, glasses, plates etc. of different metals and they sell directly in the market within the state. Manufacturers directly supply the ready material to the shopkeepers, but contractors, first receive the ready material from those to whom they give for making utensils, then supply to the shopkeepers.

Table 5.3
Work Activities in the Production Process

Work Activities	*Number*	*Percentage*
Traditional Thathiars	80	26.66
Skilled workers	97	32.34
Sellers of utensils	35	11.66
Contractors-cum-sellers	28	9.34
Contractors	23	7.66
Administrators	17	5.66
Administrators and contractors	16	5.34
Sellers of raw material	04	1.34
Total	**300**	**100.00**

Among these 9.34 per cent are performing as contractors as well as shopkeepers. In this they establish contract with traditional Thathiars and manufacturers on contract basis. After getting ready material, they sell it in the market to the wholesalers and retailers. Contractors are 7.66 per cent. They purchase raw/waste material from the market and then give it to the traditional Thathiars and manufacturers to make utensils. Contract time period depends upon the quantity of the raw material. Contractor fixes the wages according to the days at the rate of Rs 80 per day.

Other 5.66 per cent respondents perform administrative activities. They have control over the whole production process while manufacturing they are aware of every step in the production process, i.e., purchasing of raw material, selling, and supervision of workers and about quality of the material. A contractor observes over the contract process with whom he makes contract. Workers complete the contract within a limited period. All these activities are parts of utensils making process.

Difficulties in the Setting up of Work

The occupational composition of the economy is the direct reflection of its industrial composition. When industrial processes change, occupations must change. As the proportions of workers needed in a particular industry change, the proportions in the various occupations also change (Miller and Form, 1964). So, change in work organisation and occupational structure creates problems for hereditary skilled persons or other workers in setting up their work.

The main focus here is to see that the Thathiars whose hereditary occupation was not utensils making might face certain difficulties in setting up the occupation. Data reveal that out of 300 respondents 284 (94.66 per cent) respondents faced difficulties irrespective of the occupation being hereditary. Other 16 (5.34 per cent) respondents are those who started business without any difficulty. Table 5.5 shows the difficulties faced in setting up the enterprises. One of the major problems of the Thathiars is non-availability or inadequate supply of raw material (38.43 per cent), which may not be available for a long time. Lack of finance may arise at the implementation stage itself due to cost overrun. The engaged person or worker may find it difficult to get additional finance from financing institutions and unless he is able to bridge the gap, implementation will be held up. Most of the small-scale units suffer due to paucity of working capital.

Table 5.4
Difficulties Faced in Setting up the Enterprises

Difficulties	*Number*	*Percentage*
Raw material	186	38.43
Finance	186	38.43
Supervision of workers	69	14.26
Quality maintenance	43	8.88
Total	**484***	**100.00**

*Multiple Responses

Table shows that 38.43 per cent suffered due to finance. Some other difficulties they faced are primarily of workers and quality maintenance. Supervision of workers is one of the major problems in setting up of work. Every traditional worker is fully experienced in his work, especially in single kind of utensils. This creates problems for manufacturers. Skilled workers did not easily get ready to work with manufacturers or others. They want to work independently but their financial crises compel them to work with manufacturer or others. Even then, they did not agree with their policies. Quality maintenance is also one of the problems, while purchasing raw material various problems arises regarding the quality of the products. Those who start their work without any difficulty, they are financially secure and fully trained and skilled in this work. These give them proper platform to start their work without any difficulty.

Role of Hereditary Skills in Establishing Enterprises

The respondents were asked how their hereditary skills helped in establishing enterprises. Table 5.6 highlights that for most of the artisans, i.e., 27.14 per cent it was a family occupation. In the case of 21.64 per cent respondents, the business was already established by the elders, 19.20 per cent were fully experienced and trained in this work.

For others, it was more profitable business. Some joined it as economic necessity.

Table 5.5
Hereditary Skills in Establishing Enterprises

Hereditary Skills	*Number*	*Percentage*
Family occupation	89	27.14
Already established business	71	21.64
Got experience/training in the occupation	63	19.20
More profitable	56	17.08
Economic necessity	49	14.94
Total	**328***	**100.00**

*Multiple Responses

Techniques of Work and Work Organisation

From the evidence available about metals it can be said that artisans had acquired some knowledge of properties of different metals and had also become familiar with the method of preparing alloys by combining different metals, though not in ideal proportion, in order to get more useful, strong and better metal.

From the point of technological development, the evolutionary stages of metallurgy are divided into three periods (i) Native metal as stones, (ii) Native metal stage and (iii) Ore stages. The passage from one stage to another marks more and more refinement in technical skill. Thus, the main techniques used by pre-Harappan or traditional skilled man included cold or hot hammering, grinding, heating, smelting and alloying. It is admitted that these techniques were at the stage of crudeness and needed much improvement. Moreover, the variety in typology also lacked. As in the case of pottery industry, metallurgy was also at the point of initial growth, although it lagged behind the former in many respects. When development of metal technology during pre-Harappan and Harappan periods is closely examined, it becomes quiet apparent that a very spectacular improvement was made during the latter period. In other words, it was not a case of slow, gradual evolution but of sudden technological explosion. This period was truly the 'metal age' not because of abundant occurrence of metal artefacts but because of the tremendous effect of metal technology on the economics of the various Harappan industries and the growth of specialties in terms of technical know-how relating to various jobs in metal industry. It has been found that the inhabitants were not familiar with iron; instead they used other metal like copper, tin, bronze, brass, silver and gold. With them they made their utensils, weapons, tools, ornaments, toys and figurines etc. (Dahiya, 1986).

The most important metals used in India for consumption were brass (copper and zinc), bronze (copper and tin), and copper. Older descriptions refer to a greater variety of metals, but these were usually minor variations in the alloy, and were standardised over time. The metals were subjected to two basic processes: forging and casting, the products of which could be quite different. In general, forging on sheet metal tended to serve the utilitarian end of the market, whereas casting could not only render a diversified range of goods, but also produce vessels that could be decorated on the outside. The decorative skills varied, but can be reduced to two broad types: brightening the surface by polishing or plating, and designing the exterior. Designs were affected by hand: engraving on the surface, engraving on a layer of tin fixed to the exterior, or more rarely, repousse. Usually the engravings were coloured by lacquer, and that of the surface distinguished towns such as Bidar and Moradabad. Major centres of manufacture possessed both hammerers and engravers, but a few were especially well-known for their decorative work (Roy, 1996).

In the manufacture of utensils (large scale) between 1959-60 and 1962-63, the value of production fell by 25 per cent and employment by 26 per cent. In 1962-63, the production of utensils was of the order of Rs 872,000 and labour 72. In the manufacture of utensils (small-scale) between 1954-55 and 1959-60, the value of production increased by 140 per cent and employment approximately by 110 per cent. In 1962-63, 90 units were working with production worth Rs 2,639,000 and labour 392. Another feature of the industry was the introduction of the manufacture of stainless steel utensils. Brass casting is carried out both as a utilitarian industry and for ornamentation purposes. Thalis are made in copper

Fig. 5.1 Tool used by traditional Thathiars: Maganu.

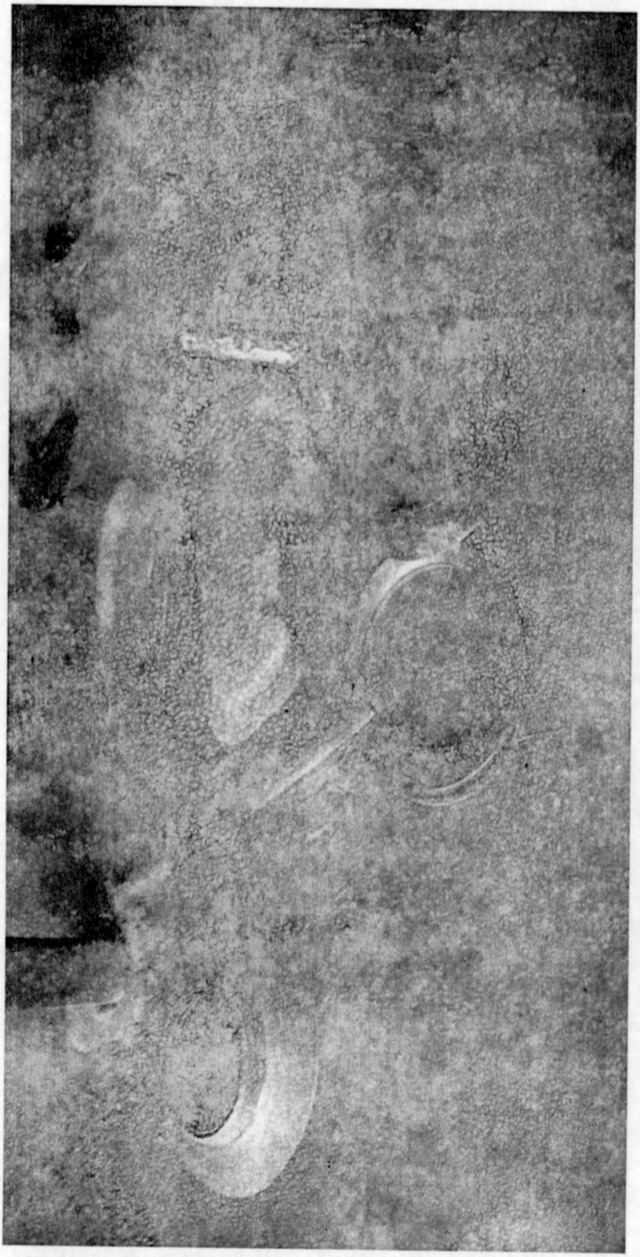

Fig. 5.2. Various Tools used in utensil making: Hammer, Sani, Moulder, Raeti, Makhu, Chisel, Chakha.

and enriched by concentric bands of ornament cast through the tin into the copper ground. Metal work as a craft is seen in the inlay work. Inlaying is done on copper and brass in floral and other designs (Datta, 1967).

As in the case of the Thathiars of Jandiala Guru, there are changes in the techniques of work with the passage of time. In the traditional times, traditional Thathiars used tools like hammers of wood and iron–Makhu (a container made of carbon soil, in big or small size), Maganu (pattern), Chaka (a round plate or structure of metal), Mekha (nails of small size), Chisel, a Hand blower etc. With the use of these tools, they applied techniques of hammering, melting, grinding, shaping to all those they would do with hands to manufacture products.

In present times, with the development and advancement of tools and with the latest improvement as in the place of (Maganu), the Thathiars are using readymade pattern for every shape of product. In the place of hand blower they use–electric furnace, electric machines for polishing and rolling machines which make metal fine. There are changes in the techniques of work. Melting is now done by modern machines, shapers are available in different pattern and grinding is done by rolling machines. Thus, the main techniques used by the Thathiars of Jandiala Guru included cold or hot work, grinding, heating, shaping and polishing. All these techniques also prevailed in pre-Harappan and Harappan periods.

Cold Work

This involves hammering done on cold metal, i.e., when the metal is below recrystalisation temperature. This gives extra hardness to the metal and thus the metal become more durable and effective.

Hot Work

Appropriate amount of hammering gives some extra hardness to the tool, but too much of it makes the metal

Fig. 5.3. Worker Melting Brass in Furnace.

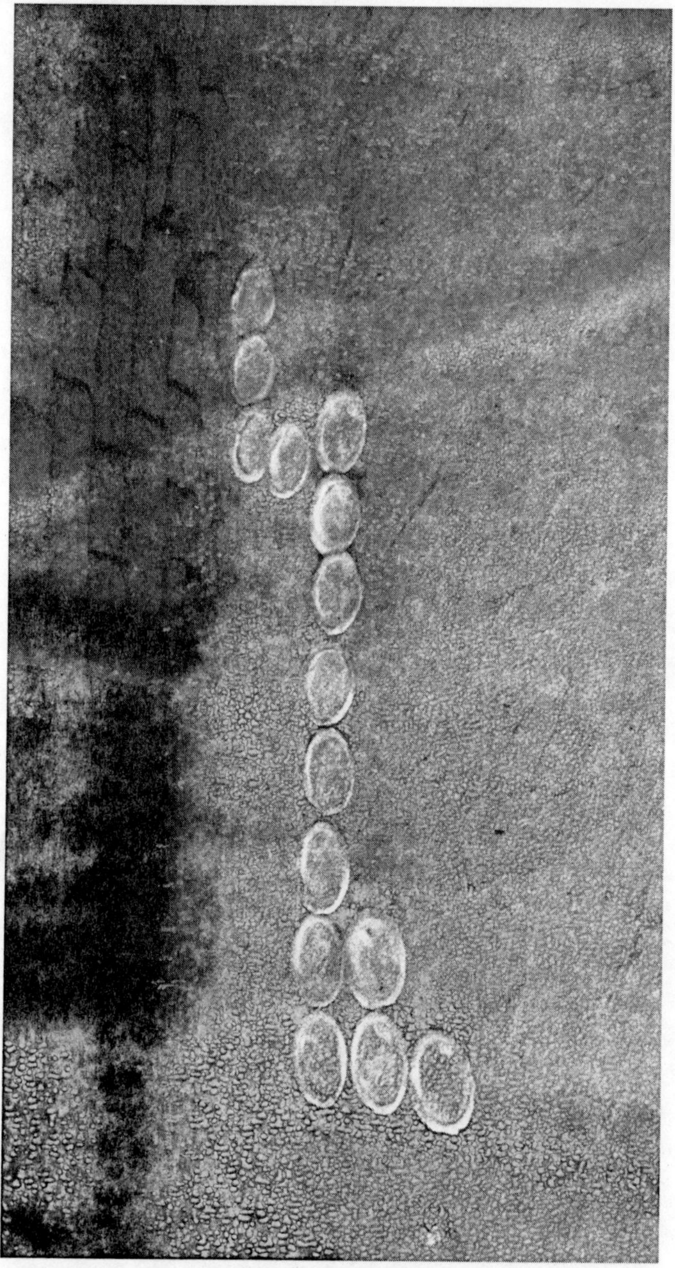

Fig. 5.4. Melted brass in clay pots.

Fig. 5.5. Rolling machine used for making metal sheets : Tale.

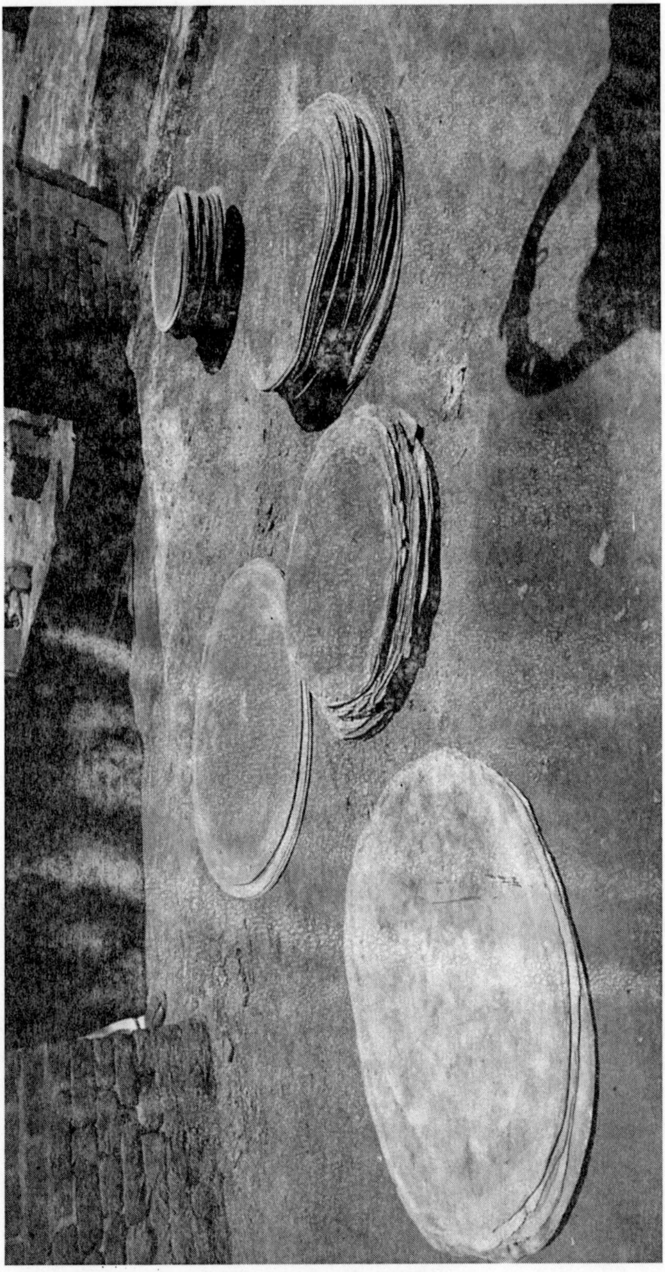

Fig. 5.6. Tale: Metal sheets.

brittle. To avoid this and to increase the density of metal it is done by closing up small pores and gas holes. In using this techniques care is taken that the metal is kept above recrystalisation point.

Hammering

Pure copper and brass vessels are manufactured by beating only, since, their shapes are simple. This technique was also used by Harappans to make deep pots and pans. In using it a flat disc of copper and bronze is placed upside down on the metal worker (Thathiar) stake. Then it is hammered and turning the metal is raised up through a series of concentric rings and finally turns into a deep pot or a pan.

Hollowing and Sinking

If the Thathiar wanted to make a shallow pan or a bowl, he used hollowing and sinking technology. In this method the metal is placed over a cup-shaped depression made either on a wooden block by hollowing it or on some other thing. Then the metal is beaten till it is sunk in the hollow and turned into shape. The Thathiars are efficient metal forgers and excellent and wonderful artists. They produced different types of utensils for domestic purposes and other kinds of things by using various different techniques.

Main Products

Metal manufacturers are perhaps the most important of all Indian art-ware. Such articles have been manufactured in this country from very ancient times. Here an attempt is made to highlight the main items produced by the Thathiars. The different types of utensil making are carried on by various people at diverse levels. Most of the household utensils in India are at the present time made of metal. They take the place of porcelain, glass and silver plate in a European household. As a matter of course rich men can alone afford to have gold and silver plate. The manufacturer of household articles in the metal is therefore limited to

Fig. 5.7. Thathiar hammering the utensils.

Fig. 5.8. Thathiar Artisan Giving Shape to Utensils on Moulder: Hollowing and Sinking.

Fig. 5.9. Degcha.

Fig. 5.10. Products Ready for Sale.

only a few places such as Haryana, Rajasthan, Varanasi, and Punjab along with Jandiala Guru which is the main market. The uses to which brass, copper and bronze are put are almost endless and the shapes and patterns of vessels made of them are often very elegant, sometimes grotesque and curious. Brass usually contains three parts of copper to one part of zinc. It is extensively used in the manufacture of plates, cups and drinking glasses. The household articles generally made of brass and mainly in readymade steel are sacrificial utensils, cooking pots, water vessels, plates, glasses and cutter etc. Every worker is not perfect in making every type of utensils. They are trained or experienced in a particular utensil.

As already discussed 69 per cent respondents are engaged in making different kinds of utensils for cooking and eating purposes. They are traditional Thathiars, manufacturers, manufacturers-cum-contractors and skilled workers. Out of these 30.47 per cent are those who are perfect in manufacturing Karahi (flat surfaced pot used to stir vegetables in the process of cooking) and Parat (a flat brass tray with a rim). Another 28.10 per cent respondents specialise in making Degcha, (a large cooking pot, broad mouthed and round with a lip) used by all classes and Degchi (smaller size than that of the Degcha). Other vessels like Gilas, Thali (plate), Kaul or Katori (bowl), Lota (metal pot) are manufactured by 18.58 per cent respondents. Only 13.80 per cent are engaged in making Patili (cooking pot), Surahi (water gaggles). Another 9.05 per cent are making decorative symbols (Waheguru, Satnam, and Khanda) in brass and in tools like small hammers of brass. Along with manufacturing they repair the vessels.

Rituals at Work

Before starting their work, every person performs some rituals. The respondents are mainly the Sikhs and Hindus. Hindus worship Mata-Vaishno and Hanuman. They fix the portraits of Mata Vaishno and other gods or goddesses in the corner of the shop. They burn incense (agarbati-dhoop) for worship. Some sprinkle holy water at work places, which they bring from temple or gurdwara. On the eve of Diwali, they light the lamps. The Sikhs recite 'Japji Sahib' and other shabads of Gurbani at their shops. Some go to gurdwara or temple daily before coming to their work places. Some go to gurdwara 'Janam Asthan Guru Baba Hundal'. Baba Hundal was Jat by caste. He remained engaged in meditation for long time and finally met the Nath Jogi. It stands for the oneness of God. Some worship "Baba Lal Ji" who was a saint. His darbar is situated at Dhyanpur in Gurdaspur district.

Working Hours

In a factory and in mechanised process the 'freedom' of an independent artisan is replaced by authority and routine. His previous existence may be governed by traditional values and responsibilities arising out of informal social relations. Punctuality, the steady and continuous effort, often removes many steps from the visible product. Having rest with reference to the clock rather than the task, are the reality of the factory, which is at marked contrast with the organisation of work in traditional life (Bal, 1995).

The Factory Act lays down the maximum number of working hours per day. No worker may be asked to work for more than eight hours a day. Among the traditional Thathiars, work starts with the rise of the sun and goes on till it gets dark. They do not have fixed working hours. It depends upon the availability of work. During Diwali festival days, they work for the whole day. In small factories or workshops they start working at 7 am and work upto 9 am in summer and 8 am to 8 am in winter with one hour lunch break. They work for 14 hours in summer and 12 hours in winter. Sometimes they work overtime. During off season they work hardly for five to six hours.

Holidays

Those who are working in a factory or workshop get one paid holiday every week, usually on Sunday, beside festival

Table 5.6

Initial and Present Investment of the Thathiars

	In Rupees	**Present Investment**						
		Below 50,000	*50,000 to 60,000*	*60,000 to 70,000*	*70,000 to 80,000*	*80,000 to 90,000*	*Above 90,000*	*Total*
Initial Investment	Below 5,000	2	1	4	18	13	00	38 (18.72)
	5,000 to 10,000	3	1	5	15	05	02	31 (15.27)
	10,000 to 15,000	3	2	16	16	25	15	77 (37.94)
	15,000 to 20,000	3	3	17	00	00	00	23 (11.33)

(Contd.)

(Contd. Table 5.7)

Initial Investment	Present Investment						
In Rupees	*Below 50,000*	*50,000 to 60,000*	*60,000 to 70,000*	*70,000 to 80,000*	*80,000 to 90,000*	*Above 90,000*	*Total*
20,000 to 25,000	2	2	1	02	02	01	10 (4.92)
25,000 to 30,000	1	2	2	04	15	00	24 (11.82)
Total	**14 (6.89)**	**11 (5.42)**	**45 (22.17)**	**55 (27.10)**	**60 (29.55)**	**18 (8.87)**	**203 (100.00)**

Figures within parenthesis indicate percentages.

holidays. All the Thathiars do not work on Vishkarma Day. The traditional Thathiars do not observe holiday even on Sunday. They do not have convention of having one day's rest in a week. But, during Diwali festival season all workshops and factory workers work even on Sundays or other holidays.

Investment

Manufacturers, traditional Thathiars, contractors and sellers invest to start their work. Most of them began with very small investments that is, with a few hundred rupees. Majority of them have depended upon their own earning to start work. Table 5.7 shows that maximum initial investment of 37.94 per cent respondents is Rs 10,000 to Rs 15,000. Only 11.82 per cent invested between Rs 25,000 to Rs 30,000.

On the other hand, 8.87 per cent respondents are those whose present investment is higher than the initial investment that is above Rs 90,000. Those who invested Rs 80,000 to Rs 90,000 are 29.55 per cent. Data reveal that their present investment in this work has raised upto lakhs of rupees. Some respondents obtained help from relatives and friends. On the other hand, 32.33 per cent are those who did not invest any money as they are engaged in other's shops.

Activities Performed by the Family Members

In a manufacturing process or handicraft work, the whole family is engaged in the production process. The traditional work used to be small in size, where very low level of technology is used perhaps due to less availability of work and capital investment and limited market opportunities. Thus, the work of the artisan remains restricted in the sense that it does not demand more hands to complete the total available work (Bal, 1995).

Data show that out of 300 respondents, 220 respondent family members are participating. Among these mainly the male members of the family participate in production process. Table 5.8 shows the exact number of family members who are engaged in the work. Mainly two to three members of the family are participating. Respondents with two family members are 30.84 per cent and with three members are 26.25 per cent which include uncle, brothers and sons. Only 10.83 per cent respondents are those whose five to six family members are working. They all may be brothers, cousin brothers, sons and grandsons.

Table 5.7
Number of Family Members Engaged

No. of Family Members	*Number*	*Percentage*
One	42	17.50
Two	74	30.84
Three	63	26.25
Four	35	14.58
Five	17	07.08
Six	09	03.75
Total	**240**	**100.00**

All these family members who are participating in work perform different kinds of activities. Among these 64 per cent are doing Thathiars' work, which involve sheet pressing, moulding, shaping, hammering and polishing. Other 17 per cent are looking after the accounts of sale and purchase and 19 per cent are engaged in contractor or managerial activities.

Participation of Women and Children

Division of labour based on sex differentiation, has given rise to three broad types of occupation. Some exclusively male, others predominantly female and the third open to both single and together (Davis, 1957). Utensil making is considered as masculine occupation, which involves a lot of physical strength. Therefore, women are not engaged in the occupation. There are mainly two reasons of non-participation of women, this is, due to heavy and manual work and secondly the social norms and values do not permit women to work.

On the other side, the children of the Thathiars generally participate in work as helpers particularly during festival seasons. They work with father in the evening or whenever they get holiday from the school. Respondents are willing to teach them the traditional skills, but do not want them to take it up as an occupation because the demand for the work involving traditional skills has considerably reduced due to modernisation.

Workers Employed

In all systems of production, there is division of labour. Labour is more finely divided in the industrial system than in any other. The emergence of manufacturing heralded a new work pattern in which the skills of the producer become less and less relevant to the final product. This development has continued in modern factories where producers are no longer regarded as people endowed with special skills but are named according to the establishment in which they work. Steel worker, textile worker, glass worker etc. are all names describing employees in different industries, irrespective of their functions and skills. All of them are designated as factory workers, industrial workers or simply workers. All these general categories reflect the changing status of the manual labour force (Hirszowicz, 1981).

Every technological change degrades certain skills while elevating the holders of other skills to the ranks of a labour aristocracy. Some technologies compel workers to live in remote communities, while other industries disperse workers in large urban conglomerations. So, industrialisation reflects upon artisan work. Artisans became or joined as workers in large production units or in factories.

Table 5.8
Workers Employed

Changes	*Number*	*Percentage*
Diversified	54	18.00
Modified	49	16.33
No change	197	65.67
Total	**300**	**100.00**

Data show that manufacturer engaged in utensil making has employed workers to carry on different activities. The range of the workers employed in the factories varies from two to twenty. Table 5.9 shows that 32.34 per cent have become skilled workers, who are fully experienced in the work, they work in other's workshops or factories. Another 23.33 per cent are daily wage workers, who work on day-to-day contract, get their wages daily. Sometimes they get raw material from manufacturers or contractors and after manufacturing, they return the ready product and get wages from the owner. Sometimes daily wagers are paid once a week. Only 9.00 per cent have become helpers, who are not fully experienced and trained in the factory work, while 35.33 per cent are those who have no employed worker participation in the work.

Wages

It is probably true that wages symbolised many irrational motives and attitudes. But the fact remains that the urban industrial working man is completely dependent on his wages, for existence and for the comfort of his family. A worker is also dependent on wages as a means of attaining non-material goals, such as status in the community (Schneider, 1957). The study reveals that a large majority of the respondents are workers. Their minimum prevailing wages are Rs 70 to Rs 300 per week which is decided according to the weight of the products produced by them. They are paid Rs 17 for one kg. Those who are working permanently are paid monthly. Their monthly wages are between Rs 2000 to Rs 3000. Only permanent workers get bonus or annual increment which is only 33 per cent of respondents. Their bonus is one per cent of the basic pay and annual increment is Rs 100 per year.

Procurement of Raw Material

Raw material is one of the basic requirements of both rural and urban artisans. Rural artisans depend upon their fixed customers. Because of financial reasons, rural artisans are unable to purchase material from market. They generally worked under the Jajmani system.

But in the case of urban artisans, they get raw material directly from market. From 1911 to 1940, traditional Thathiars depended upon government for raw material. Government made auction of the waste metal material and through auction they purchased the raw/waste material. Individually they purchased material for Rs 100 or Rs 500. Collectively or in group they purchased material with Rs 10,000 to Rs 20,000. But in recent times, the Thathiars purchase raw/waste material from local market. The main raw material for Thathiars are scrap, readymade tale (plates of metal), waste iron, silver, brass, steel-utensils and other articles, copper wires, plates of metals etc.

A large proportion of raw material is obtained by melting waste products. They purchase or get raw material from Jagadhri, Muradabad, Jammu, Benaras and local market. Those who are in manufacturing, face problems while getting raw material. They complained for the insufficient supply and non-availability of the right kinds of material. Procured material is not available at controlled prices as there are changes in prices according to the demand and seasons. Imported and scare raw material may not be available for

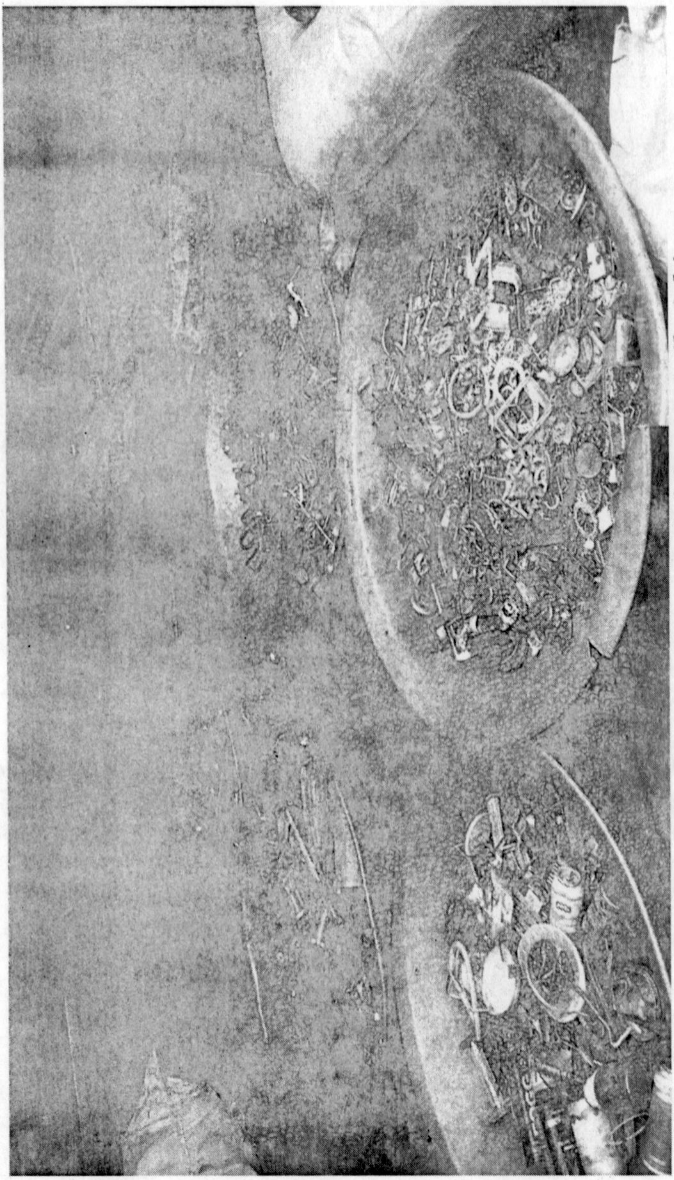

Fig. 5.11. Scrap: raw material for utensil making.

Fig. 5. 12. Pehras: used for making metal plates

a long time and when it is made available, manufacturers and contractors may be forced to purchase and store in bulk quantity to ensure regular production. In both the cases he is the loser. In the first case his production will be hampered for want of raw material and in the latter case, he has to bear the burden of heavy inventory carrying cost. Such repeated and continuous situations lead the units to sickness (Rao, 1992). General utensil manufacturer was not constrained to locate near natural raw material sources, for, in large part, the raw material used was scrap, and not ores. Copper deposits in India occur in the southern Andhra coast, Rajputana and Gujarat, along the Himalayas, Karnataka, and Chhotanagpur. It is an interesting speculation that the further back one goes, and the rarer scrap becomes, the more the industry might be seen to retreat to these areas. Remnants of this layer of manufacture, that evolved from ore smelting and had visible tribalist roots both in technologies and the artifact turned out, are still found in little hamlets scattered over some of these areas (Mukherji, 1903). The dependence on scrap did not make the industry wholly urban, but nor was brass-ware nearly as diffused or rural as textiles or leather. In general, the industry occurred in small towns and clusters of villages close to major consuming points. A list of such locations appears in the detailed accounts of the crafts prepared in the last quarter of the nineteenth century (Birdwood, 1887 and Mukherji, 1888). An important function in this scheme belonged to the peddlers who trudged the surrounding countryside exchanging, 'like the lamp-seller in Aladdin's story', new vessels for old. The poorer and the more rural the region, the wider the distance covered, the longer the periods of credit, and the riskier the business. The brazier was himself the hawker, as in certain parts of the Deccan, his travels added to the costs of production. These costs, real or monetary, would have been greater than, say, what the weaver-hawker had to bear, the finished good in brass being much bulkier. It is for these costs that concentration in towns was a strong tendency in brass. Only a few of the places appearing in the early craft monographs reappear in the mid-twentieth century, whereas most of these towns seem to have grown considerably. One inducement for increased concentration in the more recent times was a change in raw material. Foreign trade did not expose brass-ware to any significant competition, but it did substitute scrap by imported sheets to a great extent. Evidence of the direct cost-saving involved is not available, except perhaps through a minor reference in Hoey's profit-calculations for Lucknow artisans. But it is possible to believe that the gain was large. Brass sheets eliminated the need to melt the scrap in crude furnaces. Copper needing a high temperature to melt, rendered it to scale-economies which had been absent. Moreover, sheets standardised composition and quality of the metal, which were needed for mass production of utensils (Roy, 1996). Lack of raw material has direct effect on production. Low quality of material is also a problem for further processing. If raw material will be in rough condition, this will become the cause of rough pressing and finishing and this leads to low quality of the products. Transportation is also a major problem for the supply of raw material.

Sale of the Products

A convenient way of describing how market-developments altered production and exchange systems would be to see how the roles in which the three actors, dealers, *karkhanadars* and workers appear, tended to change in relation to the market, and in relation to each other. The raw material trade concentrated as a result of market expansion and easier communication. In the new role, the 'dealer' was no longer one who merely bought vessels from peddlers to forward them to the artisans, and retailing goods in turn. The dealer could now be an importer. And by switching from scrap to imported sheets the industry required that the merchants 'incur all the risks of the violent fluctuations in prices in the brass and copper markets' (Chatterjee, 1908). The dealer, further, must be wealthy enough to afford shops, spaces and godowns in the town. And since foreign inputs were not just cheaper, they were available from a world market in which price and availability were both uncertain, the dealer occasionally needed to be someone with privileged access to inputs, say, by holding licenses during both the world wars. Licenses, at the same time, were a barrier to entry for many others. An effect of increasing scale, concentration, and specialisation of capital was a sharper distinction between the biggest of the input dealers and those among the finished goods merchants. However, there were many intermediaries below them who seemed to combine both (Roy, 1996).

After completing the manufacturing process, products come in the market directly or indirectly for sale. As already discussed, 66.33 per cent respondents are engaged in the sale of the products. Out of these, 50 per cent respondents sell the products through open market, as manufacturers and traditional Thathiars sell the product directly to the shopkeepers. Another 13.34 per cent are those from whom customers themselves collect the things. They are permanent customers of the Thathiar. Other 36.66 per cent sell through agents and dealers, who play role of mediator between manufacturers, traditional Thathiars and shopkeepers, i.e., wholesalers and retailers. They sell in bulk quantity in the local market, i.e., Amritsar, Tarn Taran, Jandiala Guru, Rayya, Patti and within the state in Ludhiana, Jalandhar, Patiala, Sangrur, Gurdaspur, Ferozepur, Moga and out of the state, they sell in Jammu, Jagadhri, Ambala, Delhi, Benaras etc. The network of selling the products is quiet widespread within the state and outside the state. It may be mentioned that many of these shopkeepers are also contractors, who are of Thathiar caste. Another related interesting feature is the mode of transportation of the goods from the workers to the shops. These all are the possible variants for the shopkeepers.

Data reveal that 37 per cent respondents face problems like lower prices as the buyers do not offer fixed rate. Margins are very low 35 per cent respondents feel that market is highly competitive and due to competition price variation is very high. Only 28 per cent were those who said that demand of brass, copper and steel products is getting low, because of plastic and other material's products or utensils are available. Sometimes opposing parties create problems in marketing. They propagate against low quality and high prices of the products.

Transformation in Production Process

One of the most important aspects to access the transformation of any occupational group is to identify the changes that have taken place in the techniques of work. Same is expected in the case of Thathiars. As an occupational group, Thathiars moved towards the developed techniques of industry. Manufacturers adopt newly invented machines for work which make their work easier. The nature of workers' tasks is moulded by technological development. The division of labour between machines and aggregates of machines is the decisive factor in shaping human work, structuring social relationship and affecting the whole rhythm of individual life (Hirszowicz, 1981).

In view of Udy (1970) the main organisational transformation that must take place is a shift from socially determined to technologically determined form of work. Crucial to this shift is the institution of contractual work, its successful competition, familial, reciprocal and political work forms and its development though employer specific and job specific arrangements to a firm position in a new occupational system grounded in industrial technology (c.f. Sinha, 1990).

Techniques are specific, culturally patterned means of attaining a given end. Techniques are learnt and may require the acquisition of specialised skills. Techniques may be simple or complex. They may involve actions as in the techniques of a skilled crafts or they may be primarily intellectual, as in the case of statistical techniques (Sharma, 1992).

Change in techniques brings change in the work of artisans. Before the technological development, artisans spent a lot of time to prepare a single product. The whole process was manual. Work based on craftsmanship has certain characteristics that distinguish it from the manual labour of the modern factory. Craftsmanship was the result of a long period of apprenticeship; it implied full control by the artisan over the work process. It was characterised by variety of tasks and complex operations and it presumed the full responsibility of the producer for the final product. During the manufacturing period, which extended in England from the middle of the sixteenth century to the final third of the eighteenth century, a further evolution of technology took place. Manufacturing could generally be described as great number of workers working together at the same time and in one place in order to produce the same sort of commodity by using their manual skills under common supervision (Hirszowicz, 1981). The 'Technology of American Industry' is actually a conglomerate of many technologies derived from the requirements of particular systems of production and/or representing different stages in the development of technology (Schneider, 1957).

The eighteenth century industrial revolution of England began with the replacement of the craftsman's tools by mechanical implements. The machine entered the process of production as the world market grew larger, as labour became more divided and as better sources of power were developed. While in handicraft, workmen made use of tools, in the factory the machine makes use of man, he becomes a mere appendage of the machine (Hirszowicz, 1981). After discussing the general view about changes in techniques, as it occurred historically, it is worthwhile to focus on these changes, as they have occurred in the case of Thathiars as an artisan group. Here an attempt is made to discuss the changes introduced in the work of Thathiars, the reasons responsible to introduce change in the work process, besides the changes in techniques of work.

Changes Introduced in the Work

The Thathiar as an artisanal group has undergone transformation as a result of industrialisation, particularly with regard to change in techniques of work. Only 34.33 per cent of the total Thathiars have introduced changes. Out of these 34.33 per cent, Table 5.10 shows that 18 per cent have diversified their work and other 16.33 per cent have modified the working process. With regard to modification, respondents modified techniques of work, place of work was changed from home to outside and they joined business hands with other caste persons to gain more profits. Rest 65.67 per cent has not introduced changes because of financial problems.

Table 5.9
Changes Made in the Work

Changes	*Number*	*Percentage*
Diversified	54	18.00
Modified	49	16.33
No change	197	65.67
Total	**300**	**100.00**

Reasons Responsible to Introduce Change in Work

Further the data have been collected to know different reasons for introducing change in work. Formal and informal sources would have remained great influencing factors. Table 5.11 shows various reasons for introducing change. A proportion of (28.12 per cent) respondents, who are mainly manufacturers and contractors, introduced changes to face the competition in the market. Others (22.12 per cent) have introduced changes due to self-experience and motivation. Friends and relatives (19.82 per cent) have also remained signi cant to inspire them. Another 16.12 per cent captured over change to meet the demand of the products. Other 13.82 per cent have introduced changes to modify and improve the products. All these factors were responsible for introducing changes in work.

Table 5.10
Reasons Responsible to Introduce Change

Reasons	*Number*	*Percentage*
Competition	61	28.12
Self-experience motivation	48	22.12
Inspiration of friends and relatives	43	19.82
Demand of the product	35	16.12
For improvement	30	13.82
Total	**217***	**100.00**

*Multiple Responses

Changes in Techniques

A study of (James, 2000) depicts that several historians of both England and France have demonstrated that production was structurally transformed in various sectors of the economy by capitalism in the eighteenth and nineteenth centuries but without mechanisation of factories. The appearance of industrial capitalism without mechanisation of factories has prompted considerable rethinking about working class formation, as has an appreciation of the cultural factors involved in such formation. Christopher Johnson (1987) has observed that 'a good deal of our work as historians of the industrial transition has concerned the ways in which that vast amorphous, and ill-de ned category of handworkers called 'artisans' experienced the profound legal and economic changes of the age.

These handworkers are largely affected by the developed techniques. Among these handworker or artisan categories, the traditional Thathiar, who has developed mastery in his work, had autonomy over the complete process of production. The tools and implements which they used were inherited from ancestors and handed over to the next generation. They use very few tools. In this regard, information has been collected from the Thathiars. What kinds of tools were used by their father or grandfather? Among these tools are wooden stake for support, big and small hammer of wood, furnace or a hand blower and cutter-to cut the metal and shaper.

All these tools are still used by the Thathiars of Jandiala Guru. To know about the changing techniques of Thathiars, respondents were asked, whether they have introduced changes in the techniques of work or not? Data reveals that 48 per cent respondents did not introduce change in techniques of work. Other 52 per cent experienced changes in the techniques of work. Those Thathiars who used developed techniques in work introduced moulding machines, electric shaper, cutter, electric kilns in the work processes. The modern and electric machines made work easier, reduced physical labour of the worker, burden of work and time consumed. So, all the Thathiars have admitted that machines introduced in utensil making made the work easy. But all the workers are not able to introduce developed technology in the work processes due to financial problems.

Tools vs. Machine

Every human being does work in one form or the other. Work itself is a result of the force exerted over some distance. The elements of "force" and "distance" are usually present in the work most people do. In order to substantiate this theoretical formulation further, respondents were asked whether machines are better than tools. Sixty three per cent respondents replied that machines are better than tools, because machines are more efficient, durable, productive and profitable. Products were produced in large quantity with better durability and efficiency. Other 37 per cent respondents felt machines played negative role. They agreed that the availability of work has reduced with the mechanisation, which made them unemployed.

Political Organisation

In modern times, different aspects of an individual's life have become more clearly differentiated and he expresses each of these aspects in different associations and relationships. With the advancement in technology, the political relations have turned from simple, informal and narrow to complex, formal and wider. Data reveal that 58 per cent respondents out of the total are aware of political organisations and the rest 42 per cent are not aware of any such organisation because of lack of awareness, communication, interest and literacy. Before 1940's, there was no separate organisation for the Thathiars. When the organisations came up, it was seen that relations in these organisations are very formal and employees have joined together to improve their salary and conditions at work. As Marx (1976) argues, the trade union or the organisation of labour serves to reduce competition among workers and prevent capitalist from maximising wage exploitation, as well as serving as a medium for raising the consciousness of workers and politicising them (c.f. Bal, 1995). In these organisations, workers share common rule with other members of different castes and occupations. Data reveal that only 27 per cent respondents are members of organisations. Other 73 per cent, who are not member of the organisation, they feel these associations are not helpful to them.

At Jandiala Guru, three different types of associations have been found in which Thathiars are participating:

(i) Steel Rolling Mill Association

(ii) All India Steel Rolling Association

(iii) Thathiar Association

Mainly manufacturers, who are owners of the whole production process, know about these associations. They interact directly or indirectly. Sometimes they visit the associations' head offices. These associations are helpful to respondents to solve problems occurring in the field.

These organisations play an important role in the development of the production process. Two major processes of the occupation are, obtaining raw material and marketing of the products and for these associations–deal with local agencies, sometimes these deal with the government, in case of problems of scare resources, and finance. These associations help them to obtain loans from banks and other sources. Workers have face to face and informal type interaction with the manufacturers or owners. They can easily solve their problem mutually. Indian trade unions are yet to be organised on a sound basis. A multiplicity of small unions which are mostly organised plant-wise or firm-wise and embracing all the employers irrespective of occupational groups hardly provides a representative character to their incessant rivalry which tells upon their ability to appreciate the importance of the unity of outlook towards the problems of workers, gives the employers a latitude to exploit the situation in their favour (Mhetras, 1966). Data show that 207 (69 per cent) respondents are members of labour union. The name of the trade union is 'Thathiars Union'. Only one union has been formed by all workers of the town to meet their demands. Functioning of this union brings awareness among workers about their rights. Mostly they face problems like supply of electricity, regarding payments of wages, workers problems, disputes regarding raw material. All these problems are solved through union rather than fighting individually.

The unions function as an instrument for changing certain economic and social conditions in the factory. It fights for higher wages of workers, shorter working hours and workers' welfare. It also seeks to cut down the power of management and to enhance its own power (Schneider, 1957). In case of any dispute, the workers can always approach the union and take its help and guidance to solve it. But even then, sometimes, workers feel that the unions give rise to unnecessary disputes.

Conclusively, we may mention that a large proportion of respondents are working as traditional Thathiars or as skilled workers. Most of them started work after Indo-Pak partition. Some of them faced difficulties in the setting up of enterprises. Traditional Thathiars used traditional type of tools of wood and iron. Their present approximate investment is nearly one lakh rupees. To the maximum, six members of the family are participating. There is insufficient supply of raw material. Most of the sellers sell their products directly in the market.

This artisanal group has undergone transformation due to industrialisation, which brought modification and diversification in the work processes. They introduced changes due to various reasons like competition, demand of the products and for improvement. A small proportion of respondents introduced developed techniques and modern machines. Others are unable to use developed techniques, due to lack of resources. Majority of the respondents think machines are better than tools. Before the technological advancement an artisan spent a lot of time and physical labour on manufacturing a single thing. Machines have multiple qualities which make the work less time consuming, and more comfortable and easier. Due to improvement and awareness among workers, their relationships with the employers have become complex.

6

Occupational Mobility

In the previous chapter various processes of work of the Thathiars have been discussed. It also discusses changes, which have taken place in the occupational structure due to industrialisation and technological development. This technological development introduced machines in the work processes, which brought changes in the nature of Thathiars' work. This gave rise to new combinations of work activities, i.e., manufacturers, contractors, wholesalers, retailers, manufacturers-cum-contractors, contractors-cum-shopkeepers and skilled workers. The study reveals that due to changes in the work processes, many of the traditional Thathiars have joined factories as skilled workers and also in other occupations related with utensil making.

In the present Chapter, discussion is focused on occupational mobility experienced by the Thathiars. This refers to the movement of individuals, families or groups from one occupation to another. It is considered to be a good measure of social mobility by sociologists. It reflects the fact as to what extent a social system and the associated economy are open or rigid (Singh, 1986). Studies of occupational mobility generally have been of two types: (1) inter-generational comparisons of occupations, and (2) occupational career studies of individuals. In the first type, the occupation of the individual is compared with that of his father, and in some instances, with that of his grandfather as well. In the second, the several occupations held by an individual in his work history are compared. Both types of studies rely upon occupational groupings assumed to be arranged in a hierarchy, grouped either as manual and non-manual occupations, or by census type categories as professional, managerial, skilled and so on.

Those of the first type are intended to measure and document the extent to which the father's occupation has determined the son's occupation. If the two are consistently similar throughout the sample studied, then the presumption is that little mobility has taken place. If, on the contrary, the son's occupation differs from that of his father's mobility—upward or downward—is presumed to be evidenced (Reissman, 1959).

The focus here is on the intergenerational occupational mobility, intragenerational occupational mobility, which shows the occupational structure of grandfather, father and respondent generation. Besides this, place from where they carry the work, reasons for joining the work, interest of children in this occupation, changes in the occupation of family members have been discussed.

Many different sets of occupational categories have been devised for sociological studies. One that is widely used is the set of categories utilised by Richard Centers: business executives, professionals, small businessmen, white-collar workers, semi-skilled manual workers and unskilled manual workers (Sharma, 1992).

Mobility is generally approached from a number of dimensions, one such dimension is the time phase of mobility. Here, intergenerational mobility can be distinguished from intragenerational mobility, even though the two forms can exist simultaneously for individuals and collectivities.

A second dimension of mobility involves its direction. Three separate but often related directional axis can be identified. The most commonly analysed is vertical mobility, movement up or down in the stratification system. A second axis is a change in social function that does not involve a change in status or horizontal mobility. The third axis is spatial mobility, change in the location of the occupation. While each of this axis is analytically distinct, they are frequently related in reality. Each also plays an important role in intergenerational and intragenerational mobility (Hall, 1975).

The contemporary occupational structure reflects the state of the technology involved in various occupations. With the advent of industrialisation, the nature of occupations undergoes change. The growth of industry is no longer marked by increasing numbers of manual labourers. Moore (1967) elaborates on this point by noting that the change in occupational structure during development actually involves five related processes. The first of these is that workers become involved in market participation. Rather than existing on a simple subsistence level, both agricultural and industrial workers participate in the labour and financial markets. The second process is what Moore calls, 'sectoral relocation'. This refers to a shift of occupational sites away from subsistence agriculture toward economic production in industry or agriculture. As this occurs, there may be heightened unemployment, since many traditional handicraft operations are no longer needed and the workers are not absorbed into the new industrial system. The additional processes during industrialisation are the upgrading of skill requirements in the labour force, specialisation of occupation and greater status mobility, both within and between generations. These processes in the industrialising societies are similar to those that have occurred in societies that have already passed through the period of industrialisation (c.f. Hall, 1975).

Intergenerational Occupational Mobility

Intergenerational occupational mobility refers to the mobility in occupational choices between household members in successive generations. In this mobility, the occupation of the individual is compared with that of his father and with that of his grandfather. Occupational differences in these two generations show occupational mobility. The mobility helps a lot to understand changes in social sphere and its direction in present society. A few studies have focused on intergenerational choices for a set of variables including occupation. For example, Hnatkovska, Lahiri, and Paul (2013) study intergenerational choices for educational attainment, industry of employment, income and occupational choices. Comparing levels of intergenerational educational mobility and intergenerational occupational mobility, Majumder (2010) finds educational mobility to be more prevalent than occupational mobility across generations in India. Fewer studies have focused exclusively on intergenerational occupational choices. In these, the attempt has generally been to describe the presence of intergenerational occupational mobility in India. For example, Kumar, Heath, and Heath (2002b) and Singh and Motiram (2012) find persistence rather than mobility to be the norm for intergenerational occupational choices.

In this study a large proportion of respondents are those, whose fathers and grandfathers were in utensil making. In the traditional times, the whole process of production was manual which was quiet tough. Hammering, melting, grinding, shaping that is every step depended on physical labour and took long time to prepare a single product. They used traditional tools of wood and iron. With the passage of time, when industrialisation took place every process underwent change, which influenced the ways of performing work. Introduction of modern machines made the work easier and increased the capacity of production. Due to the changes in the work processes, the work has been diversified.

Table 6.1
Intergenerational Occupational Mobility from Grandfather to Father

Last Occupation of Grandfather

Occupations	*Traditional Thathiars*	*Manufacturers*	*Wholesalers of Utensils*	*Shops of Utensil's Raw Material*	*Contractors*	*Retail Shops of Utensils*	*Skilled Workers*	*Kiryana / General Shops*	*Fruits and Vegetable Shops*	*Total*
Traditional Thathiars	187	1	-	-	-	9	24	15	10	246 (82.00)
Kaseras	2	-	2	-	1	2	2	-	-	9 (3.00)
Thathiars and Kaseras	1	1	1	1	-	1	-	-	-	5 (1.66)
Thathiars and Contractors	1	1	1	1	1	1	-	-	-	6 (2.00)

(Contd.)

(Contd. Table 6.1)

Last Occupation of Grandfather

Occupations	*Traditional Thathiars*	*Manufacturers*	*Wholesalers of Utensils*	*Shops of Utensil's Raw Material*	*Contractors*	*Retail Shops of Utensils*	*Skilled Workers*	*Kiryana / General Shops*	*Fruits and Vegetable Shops*	*Total*
Hawkers of Utensils	1	-	-	-	1	-	-	2	-	4 (1.34)
Kiryana Shops	-	-	-	-	-	2	-	13	5	20 (6.66)
Hawkers of Clothes	-	-	-	-	-	-	5	-	1	6 (2.00)
Tea Stall	-	-	-	-	-	-	4	-	-	4 (1.34)
Total	**192 (64.00)**	**3 (1.00)**	**4 (1.34)**	**2 (0.66)**	**3 (1.00)**	**15 (5.00)**	**35 (11.66)**	**30 (10.00)**	**16 (5.34)**	**300 (100.00)**

Figures within parenthesis indicate percentage.

People have moved towards the other occupations related to Thathiar work, which are less manual and non-manual.

Table 6.1 shows 90.66 per cent grandfathers and 84.66 per cent fathers were engaged in this work. Among these 82 per cent grandfathers and 64 per cent fathers were traditional Thathiars. This shows father's generation has moved to other occupations as compared to grandfather's generation. Other occupations in utensil making are in a small proportion.

But, in father's generation, the rate of mobility in other occupations of utensil making was higher than grandfather generation. In grandfather's time, Kaseras were 3 per cent, Thathiar and Kaseras (shopkeepers) in the combined process only 1.66 per cent were engaged. Only 2 per cent were in Thathiar and contractor's job. Hawkers of utensils were 1.34 per cent. These proportions show occupational structure of grandfather's generation while 10 per cent were in other occupations, i.e., kiryana shops, hawkers of clothes and petty shopkeepers.

In father's generation, a large proportion was of traditional Thathiars, but the movement from traditional Thathiar work to other occupations related to utensil making was highest which is from 8 per cent to 20.66 per cent. These changes were the result of transformation and use of developed or modern techniques of work. With the advent of machines, manufacturers took over which led to other categories of workers like skilled workers and contractors in this occupation.

The proportion of manufacturers was only 1 per cent, wholesalers and retailers were 6.34 per cent, and raw/waste material shops were only 0.66 per cent. In this generation, 11.66 per cent fathers joined as skilled workers, who were mainly in traditional Thathiar work. This shows horizontal mobility in the work. As a skilled worker, they earned more. Tough activities were performed by modern machines, which

Table 6.2
Intergenerational Occupational Mobility from Father to Son Present Occupation of Respondents

Last Occupation of Father

Occupations	*Traditional Thathiars*	*Manufacturers*	*Manufacturers and Contractors*	*Wholesalers of Utensils*	*Shops of Utensil's Raw Material*	*Contractor / Shops of Utensils*	*Contractor*	*Retail Shopkeeper of Utensils*	*Skilled Workers*	*Total*
Traditional Thathiars	68 (22.66)	13	9	3	2	15	14	16	52	192 (64.00)
Manufacturers	-	2	1	-	-	-	-	-	-	3 (1.00)
Wholesalers of Utensils	-	-	-	2	-	1	1	-	-	4 (1.34)
Shops of Utensil's Raw Material	-	-	-	-	2	-	-	-	-	2 (0.66)
Contractor	2	-	1	-	-	-	-	-	-	3 (1.00)

(Contd.)

(Contd. Table 6.2)

Last Occupation of Father / *Occupations*	*Traditional Thathiars*	*Manufacturers*	*Manufacturers and Contractors*	*Wholesalers of Utensils*	*Shops of Utensil's Raw Material*	*Contractor / Shops of Utensils*	*Contractor*	*Retail Shopkeeper of Utensils*	*Skilled Workers*	*Total*
Contractor	2	-	1	-	-	-	-	-	-	3 (1.00)
Retails Shops of Utensils	3	-	3	2	-	2	1	4	-	15 (5.00)
Skilled Workers	3	2	2	2	-	3	5	6	12	35 (11.66)
Karyana / General Shops	2	-	-	-	-	5	1	-	22	30 (10.00)
Petty Shopkeeper	2	-	-	-	-	2	1	-	11	16 (5.34)
Total	**80 (26.66)**	**17 (5.66)**	**16 (5.34)**	**9 (3.00)**	**4 (1.34)**	**28 (9.34)**	**23 (7.66)**	**26 (8.66)**	**97 (32.34)**	**300 (100.00)**

Figures within parenthesis indicate percentage.

reduced their physical labour. In this generation, 15.34 per cent were in other occupations, i.e., karyana, general and petty shopkeepers. The rate of mobility of joining other occupations rather than Thathiar work was higher than that of the grandfathers' generation due to the changes in the consumption pattern of the people.

The information collected about the last occupation of grandfathers and fathers indicate that, 187 persons were common, who were traditional Thathiars, which is 62.33 per cent, involved in traditional work. But with the passage of time changes have been introduced in the work processes of utensil making.

On the other hand, Table 6.2 shows the mobility between father and son (respondent) generations. Data reveal that 26.66 per cent respondents and 64 per cent fathers are in traditional Thathiar work. Difference of these proportions show that a majority of respondents moved to the other occupations of utensils making. Among these two generations, 22.66 per cent are common, who are traditional Thathiars. On the other hand when industrialisation took place, one per cent joined as manufacturers in fathers' generation and respondents are 5.66 per cent, who are in manufacturing. Wholesalers were 1.34 per cent in father generation and at present 3 per cent respondents are in this work. Father's generation indicates that retailers were 5 per cent and now respondents' generation has 8.66 per cent. Shops of utensil raw/waste material were 0.66 per cent in father generation and presently 1.34 per cent respondents are engaged in it. Even the proportion of contractors has increased from 1 per cent to 7.66 per cent in respondent's generation. Skilled workers in father generation were 11.66 per cent but now their proportion has increased three times, i.e., 32.33 per cent have become skilled worker in small-scale factories and workshops. Thus, the comparison of these generations indicates the rate of mobility in various work activities of utensil making from time to time.

Place of Carrying Work Activities

Table 6.3 reveals that a large proportion of grandfathers (68.88 per cent) and fathers (72.44 per cent) have been carrying on their work from the same place, i.e., Jandiala Guru. They mentioned that from the very early age of life when they were school going children, they were observing this work. They feel this work is in their blood. They are carrying it on from forefathers and from the same place, where they took birth. A very small proportion of 15.93 per cent grandfathers and 14.96 per cent fathers carried this work from outside Punjab, i.e., from Muradabad, Delhi, Jagadhri, and Benaras. Other 15.19 per cent grandfathers and 12.60 per cent fathers migrated from Pakistan due to Indo-Pak partition. They carried their work from Pakistan, i.e., Gujranwala, Rawalpindi, Maksuda, Islamabad, Gujarkala. Among these Gujranwala and Islamabad were the famous places for Thathiars' work.

Table 6.3
Place of Carrying Work Activities

Place	*Grandfather*	*Father*	*Total*
Same Town	186 (68.88)	184 (72.44)	370 (70.61)
At different places in India	43 (15.93)	38 (14.96)	81 (15.45)
At different places in Pakistan (Before Partition)	41 (15.19)	32 (12.60)	73 (13.94)
Total	**270 (51.52)**	**254 (48.48)**	**524 (100.00)**

Figures within parenthesis indicate percentage.

Intragenerational Occupational Mobility

To know about the intragenerational occupational mobility, query has been made to find out the details of the occupations held by the respondents. For analysis, the very first occupation and the present occupation have been taken into consideration. It has been found in Table 6.4 that present occupation of 26.66 per cent respondents is traditional Thathiar. In other occupations too there are changes. Those whose first occupation was manufacturing, with the passage of time, they started contractor's work along with manufacturing process. Some became wholesalers from retailers etc. This shows horizontal mobility in the occupational structure of Thathiars. These changes are the result of modernisation, transformation and awareness among workers. Every person wants to earn more for better life which motivates him to join better work of choice.

It has been found that 25.34 per cent respondents remained stagnant to the traditional Thathiar work. On the other side a large proportion of respondents changed the first occupation and joined the other occupation in utensil making.

The proportion of traditional Thathiar work is low, as from 55 per cent respondent's first occupation as traditional Thathiar, it has now come down to 26.66 per cent. This shows a pattern of mobility in this work. There is increase in the proportion of manufacturers, contractors, retail shopkeepers of utensils and skilled workers. Majority of them have joined as skilled worker, which is 32.34 per cent, because industrialisation changed the work processes. This gave rise to the modification/diversification of the occupation. Most of the traditional Thathiars think that it's better to work in others' workshops rather than working independently. Because, the raw material is expensive, they are not in a position to afford modern technology or machinery. That's why they have joined as skilled workers.

Besides this 17.34 per cent respondents are those whose first occupations were retail shops of clothes, karyana or general shops. But the popularity and increase in the demand of metal products motivated them to join this

Table 6.4
Intragenerational Occupational Mobility from Father to Son Present Occupation of Respondents

First Occupation of Respondent — *Occupations*	*Traditional Thathiars*	*Manufacturers*	*Manufacturers and Contractors*	*Wholesalers of Utensils*	*Shops of Utensil's Raw Material*	*Contractor / Shops of Utensils*	*Contractors*	*Retail Shopkeeper of Utensils*	*Skilled Workers*	*Total*
Traditional Thathiar	76 (25.34)	7	5	3	2	3	10	11	48	165 (55.00)
Manufacturers	-	5	1	1	-	2	-	-	-	9 (3.00)
Wholesalers of Utensils	-	-	2	-	-	5	1	-	-	8 (2.66)
Shops of Utensil's Raw Material	-	1	-	-	2	-	-	-	-	3 (1.00)
Contractors	1	2	2	-	-	1	-	-	-	6 (2.00)

(Contd.)

(Contd. Table 6.4)

	Occupations	*Traditional Thathiars*	*Manufacturers*	*Manufacturers and Contractors*	*Wholesalers of Utensils*	*Shops of Utensil's Raw Material*	*Contractor / Shops of Utensils*	*Contractors*	*Retail Shopkeeper of Utensils*	*Skilled Workers*	*Total*
First Occupation of Respondent	Retails Shops of Utensils	2	2	2	2	-	-	1	5	4	18 (6.00)
	Skilled Workers	1	-	1	1	-	8	4	4	20	39 (13.00)
	Retail Shops of Clothes	-	-	2	1	-	5	5	3	17	33 (11.00)
	Karyana/ General Shops	-	-	1	1	-	4	2	3	8	19 (6.34)
	Total	**80 (26.66)**	**17 (5.66)**	**16 (5.34)**	**9 (3.00)**	**4 (1.34)**	**28 (9.34)**	**23 (7.66)**	**26 (8.66)**	**97 (32.34)**	**300 (100.00)**

Figures within parenthesis indicate percentage.

occupation. Some of them are those whose fathers were in this occupation but they did not join or take it as first occupation, but later they joined the hereditary occupation.

Comparison of Tables 6.1 and 6.4 shows the four marginal distributions of occupations i.e., last occupation of grandfather (GF: LO) and father (F: LO), first occupation of son (S: FO) and son's present occupation (S: PO). Here the

Table 6.5
Intergenerational Profiles of Grandfather, Father and Son

OCCUPATIONS	*GF:LO*	*F:LO*	*S:FO*	*S:PO*
Traditional Thathiars (TT)	246	192	165	90
Kaseras	9	-	-	-
TT + Kaseras	5	-	-	-
TT+ Contractors	6	-	-	-
MAINELY OWN- ACCOUNT PRODUCTION (OAP)	**266**	**192**	**165**	**80**
Contractors	-	3	6	23
Wholesalers: Utensils	-	4	8	9
Hawkers: Utensils	4	-	--	-
Retailers: Raw materials of utensils	-	2	3	4
Contractors of Utensils		15	18	26
Retailers of Utensils	-	-	-	28
MARKETING OF PRODUCTS	**4**	**24**	**35**	**90**
Retailers: Fruits/Vegetables	-	16	-	-
Retailers: Clothes	-	-	33	-
Hawkers: Clothes	6	-	-	-
Tea Stalls	4	-	-	-
General Shop (Karyana)	20	30	19	NIL
CONSUMER GOODS MARKET	**30**	**46**	**52**	**-**
Manufacturers	-	3	9	17
Manufacturers and Contractors	-	-	-	16
Skilled Workers	-	35	39	97
MAINELY PRODUCTION BY WAGE LABOUR(WLP)	**-**	**38**	**48**	**130**
TOTAL	**300**	**300**	**300**	**300**

Source :Tables 6.1 and 6.4.

objective will be to compare the four marginal distributions of occupations—GF: LO, F: LO, S: FO and S: PO. Organise the occupations by following the underlying logic (i.e., by "species" in place of "tree" individually) and in this case, let us have "employment status" as the underlying logic. That way, we get the picture of profile of mobility as shown in the Table 6.5. This table clearly brings out the indication of emergence of class within the caste. Traditional family base (OAP) is dwindling-giving space to market-based employer-employee relationship (WLP).

Reasons for Change in the Work of the Respondents

According to this study, respondents are indulging in various occupations of utensil making. From traditional work to modern industrial work this passage introduces changes in various activities, which make work easy. The data reveal that 46 respondents are those whose fathers were not in this Thathiar work. They have changed the occupation than his father and join Thathiar work.

Table 6.6
Reasons for Change in the Work of the Respondents

Reasons	*Number*	*Percentage*
To Earn More	38	27.53
Improved Working Condition	37	26.82
More Profitable	34	24.64
Less Manual Work	29	21.01
Total	**138***	**100.00**

*Multiple Responses

Table 6.6 shows the reasons as to why respondents change their work. As 27.53 per cent joined this to earn more, 26.82 per cent due to improved working condition, with the advancement and modernisation, 24.64 per cent joined this because they realised it will be more profitable work than the other ones. While 21.01 per cent, joined this because it involved less or non-manual work introduced in the work process like contractor, shopkeeper, etc. These were the reasons which motivated respondents to take up this occupation, which was different from that of their father's.

Interest of Children in this Work

With the changing sphere, every aspect undergoes change. Change in taste and choice of occupation etc. brings change in traditional life from time to time. The study reveals that 77.66 per cent children are not interested in this work. Table 6.7 shows the multiple responses of lack of interest. Nearly 30 per cent said that demand is decreasing as plastic and other material is taking place of metal utensils. Response of 25.20 per cent is that this work is less pro□table. Other 37.59 per cent are not interested because of manual work and lower status. A small proportion of children, that is, 6.59 per cent are not interested because of the level of their education.

Table 6.7
Response of Uninterested Children

Reasons	*Number*	*Percentage*
Demand in Decreasing	79	30.62
Less Pro□table	65	25.20
Manual Work	58	22.48
Lower Status	39	15.11
Children are educated	17	06.59
Total	**258***	**100.00**

*Multiple Responses

On the other hand, a less proportion of children which is 22.35 per cent are interested to join this traditional work.

They think, "This is one of the traditional occupations, which would never vanish. This gives us identification." Some interested due to hereditary occupation. They said that this occupation is their means of livelihood and we worship our occupation. Some are engaged in some well established business wherein their earning is good. They have modified work with the advent of modern techniques.

Change in Traditional Occupation

The study reveals that 276 family persons have changed the traditional occupation. Among these family members are brothers, uncles, cousins and nephews. They joined other occupations like general store, work on other's shops or stores, karyana shop, accountancy, teaching and legal profession.

Table 6.9 reveals that the reasons for change in traditional occupations are, demand of metal utensils is less or decreasing, (23.89 per cent). Other 21.81 per cent joined other occupation to earn more, 16.63 per cent were not interested in traditional occupation. Another 27.79 per cent changed this occupation because of its being manual and noisy work. Only 9.88 joined other occupations due to good academic qualification.

To sum up, occupational mobility shows various directions of change in occupation. Intergenerational occupational mobility generates a comparison between the occupation of grandfather, father and son. This study describe that there is horizontal mobility in the occupation of the Thathiars. It has happened due to changes introduced in work process. Most of the fathers and grandfathers carried their work from different places in India and Pakistan.

The intragenerational occupational mobility, show less mobility rate in traditional Thathiar work. Respondents move to other occupations which are less manual and reduced physical labour. These occupations are like manufacturer, contractor, shops of wholesalers, retailers

Table 6.8
Nature of Present Occupation of Respondent's Relatives

Relation → *Occupation* ↓	*Brother*	*Uncle*	*Cousin*	*Nephew*	*Total*
General Store	21	10	15	18	64 (23.18)
Work on Other's Workshop	12	24	08	15	59 (21.38)
Karyana's Shop	21	10	14	04	49 (17.76)
Accountant	17	18	06	03	44 (15.94)
Teaching	12	09	12	10	43 (15.58)
Legal Profession	04	02	04	07	17 (06.16)
Total	**87 (31.53)**	**73 (26.45)**	**59 (21.37)**	**57 (20.65)**	**276 (100.00)**

Figures within parenthesis indicate percentage.

Table 6.9
Reasons for Change in Occupation

Reasons	*Number*	*Percentage*
Demand of metal utensils is less	92	23.89
To earn more	84	21.81
Not interested in traditional occupation	64	16.63
Manual work	56	14.55
Noisy work	51	13.24
Level of education	38	09.88
Total	**385***	**100.00**

*Multiple Responses

etc. A large majority joined as a skilled worker, the rate of mobility is highest in this job. They themselves feel secure to join as skilled workers. A large proportion of children of the respondents are not interested in this work. Even most of the respondents' relatives have changed the traditional occupation and have joined other occupations rather than Thathiar work.

7

Conclusions

The industrial mode of production began some 250 years ago in Britain and from there it spread to the entire world. In the simplest sense an industrial society is a social system whose mode of production focuses primarily on finished goods manufactured with the aid of machinery (www.sociologyguide.com). For most of the twentieth century historians have debated, often heatedly, the process of industrialisation from mid-eighteenth century well into the twentieth century. Industrialisation had powerful impact on artisans and handicrafts production. It can be observed in terms of various dimensions. The demand for new goods and services have been created. The introduction of new technology in agricultural sector requires new skills, which generally artisans lack. Industries produced the standardised products in bulk, with greater efficiency and their commodities are cheaper and more durable than the artisan products. All these processes have affected the artisans adversely (Bal, 1995).

The artisans may be divided into rural and urban according to their nature of work and activities performed. The rural artisans are masons, carpenters, blacksmiths, potters, weavers etc. who are directly related with agriculture and the families of farmers for household articles. The urban artisans are mainly the utensil-makers, goldsmiths, weavers, tanners, dyers, painters, and carpenters as they had demand for their work in urban areas. Both of these types of artisans were in great demand for their monopoly over certain skills. But now the growth of industries has come up as a strong competitor against them.

The experience of Europe shows that the effect of industrialisation during the late eighteenth and nineteenth centuries fundamentally transformed the artisanary of Europe's cities. Multiple forces like legal, political, intellectual, demographic and economic converged during the era of industrialisation and one such result was the destruction of the culture of the artisans and the transformation of their identity.

The impact of industrial development varies from one country to another and on one artisan group to another. Some of the artisan groups have been destroyed completely while others could survive by reutilising their skills through the industries (Bal, 1995). A study conducted by Sharma (1986) proposed that the process of industrialisation in the area of leather work would become an instrument of socio-economic development and consequently of social mobility for the artisans belonging to the Chamar caste. Though, shoe-making is carried out by the Chamar caste, yet trading in shoes and other leather items has no longer remained in their domain. It has now been increasingly taken over by other business communities, such as Banias, Khatris and even Brahmins. In fact, men of high castes have monopolised the leather business as owners and employers to a great extent as it. This is a paying business in pecuniary terms. Shoe-making has also acquired the status of an organised occupation having its own market at local, regional, national and international levels. It has helped in the survival of traditional skills and has created the demand for the same in the market situation. The changes occurring in the position of the occupation as such have become a major motivating factor for the Chamar artisans to adopt shoe-making as their career.

The present study shows the reverse of the assumed consequences of industrialisation. The Thathiars have diversified and modified their work with the advent of machinery. But due to the lack of the demand of metal products and tough nature of work, they have joined other occupations rather than utensil making. Similarly, a study on "The Artisans of Benaras" by Kumar (1988) indicates that the brass and copper industry forms a contrast with the silk industry in that it has been in progressively troubled straits for the past seventy to eighty years. Of those working at utensils of one kind or another, approximately 50 per cent have left the occupation in the last thirty to fifty years judging by information from individual families. As the Royal Commission on Labour noted in 1931, artisans worked for long hours, but this did not signify a busy market. The metal utensils industry was 'steadily going down and the men whose ancestors had been engaged in it for generations have to work harder and harder to eke out their existence.

Shukla and Anima study (1981) have shown the continuity as well as change in the occupation of artisans. Bose's (1982) study has focused on various features of production organisation and market relations of potters of Gujarat. Another study of traditional potters by Krishnan (1989) depicts that potters are producers and the market is central factor in their life and work. A study conducted by Bal (1995) on blacksmiths as an occupational group shows that the powerful forces of industrialisation have weakened the bond of caste with occupation. With the technological development, people from high castes crossed the caste barriers and have taken to the smithy.

Sharma's study (1996) on, "Artisans of the Punjab" reveals that change of occupations by artisans in the early stages was largely towards agriculture and later on towards industry where they could employ their skills and energies more effectively and advantageously. These changes, however, did not appreciably help them to improve their social evaluation. They continued to be evaluated with reference to their caste which remained the source of frustration and discontent. The increasing educational opportunities provided other avenues for change to the disoriented and discontented artisans.

Parathasarathy's study (1999) "Artisan of Gujarat", indicate that majority of the artisan households in the study reported that there has not been any change in the type of products made during the previous decade, though a signi cant proportion of the households of potters, shoe-makers and carpenters reported discontinuation of the production of some of the goods produced by them previously. Douglas' study (2006) on weavers, artisan-capitalist and the transformation of the informal economy (1940-1960) indicates that they were able to expand the realm of their economic activities in great part because of the new power they had acquired in the artisanal towns of western India. State actors depended upon them to win elections and to generate support for projects of economic development. The informal economy in short depended upon the emergence of a particular political order. The explosive growth of the "decentralised" sector in textiles after the period covered here was possible because this order was already in place by the early 1960s. Increasingly, new forms of merchant capital poured into textile production in places like Surat and Bhiwandi.

The major ndings of the present study conducted on an artisan group—the Thathiars in an urban centre, Jandiala Guru in Amritsar District, help us to understand the process of transformation amongst them. The Thathiar is that man who sells and makes vessels of copper, bronze, brass and other mixed metals. They have experienced transformation due to advancement and transformation in the work processes. Especially, with the advent of industrialisation, they experienced change in the nature of their work, occupation and caste status.

The industrialisation has made the structure of the society more open and flexible. People are leaving the caste ascribed occupations and taking to the occupations of their own choice. There have emerged more opportunities for occupational mobility. The findings of this study are that most of the respondents were born at the same place, i.e., Jandiala Guru, other were migrated from Delhi, Jagadari and Western Punjab that became part of Pakistan after partition. Out of those who were displaced due to partition, small proportion were those whose hereditary occupation was utensil making. Others joined due to availability of this work. Before migration they were carrying on various activities, such as general merchants, karyana shopkeepers and factory workers.

With the impact of industrialisation the traditional association between caste and occupation is disintegrating. The nature of their work determined the status in caste hierarchy. Thathiars, because of the nature of their work, and the services they provided to others have been appended to the artisan castes and carried backward caste status in the caste hierarchy. Contrarily, they mythically claimed to have a Khatri status. They have constructed various myths sharing their divine association with the persons of high castes and eventually they claim to have had a Khatri caste, i.e., a traditionally trading caste ranked high in the caste hierarchy. In a way, this artisan caste could be one of the illustrations of the sanskritisation process.

As a result of the Green Revolution and its consequences on the lives of the people on the one hand and the availability of machine made utensils in the urban and rural market on the other transformed the lives of the traditional Thathiars.

The respondents have also narrated that in the 1950s the poor working and living conditions led them to approach Partap Singh Kairon, the Chief Minister of Punjab, asking for a backward caste status, which entitled them to get quota for raw material - the expensive metals, reservation in government jobs, scholarships for children for studies etc. Therefore, for all purposes of enumeration, Thathiars were taken as backward caste. Interestingly, at present, as this study reveals, all thc respondents have mentioned 'Khatri' as their caste.

As the benefits of the Green Revolution percolated to all sections of the society, the Thathiars also experienced the possibilities of diversification in their traditional work. They introduced changes in the work. Some of them started manufacturing units; some took to contractual work, others to the sale of the utensils. Many of the traditional artisans joined factories as skilled workers. The change in their work made them economically better off than before. There is a reasonable basis to argue that this economic change brought in them the aspirations for claiming higher caste status.

Also, over the time, introduction of other materials like glass, plastic and porcelain has changed the taste and needs of the people. This led to reduction in the demand of metal products. Moreover, the younger generation is no more interested in this work. They think that this work carries lower status. The work is noisy and physically tough and hard as compared to other kinds of work. They have started taking to other kinds of jobs/occupations rather than utensil making. Due to change in their occupation, they consider themselves as Khatri by caste (which is high trading caste). The reason which they gave is that now they are not in the occupation of the Thathiar caste, which was backward; therefore, they ceased to be Thathiars. By adopting other trading occupations, they have started claiming the status of Khatris. The pattern of their mobility is associated with the changed nature of the occupation.

Kuppuram's study (2002) brings out the inherent limitations of Indian artisans in the wake of industrial development. Though the Indian artisans could produce goods of exceptional quality, much of Indian manufacturing was highly labour intensive. The Indian artisans used a variety of tools and implements in facilitating their manufacturing. But there was an insufficient investment in augmenting and expanding the range of labour - saving tools. Therefore, as a result of industrial development, India had a very large pool of relatively cheap skilled labour trained in a variety of special tasks. India's great manufacturing strengths thus became a significant obstacle in transitioning towards the modern industrial era (sahistory.html).

Technology has an obvious effect on individual freedom, in some ways increasing it, in others restricting it. However, since capitalism is a social system based on inequalities, it does not develop in a social vacuum. In a capitalist society, technologies useful to the rich and powerful are generally the ones that spread and consolidate. It can be seen from capitalist industry where technology has been implemented specifically to deskill the worker, so replacing the skilled, valued craftsperson with the easily trained (and eliminated) "mass worker". In Proudhon's words, the "machine, or the workshop, after having degraded the labour by giving him a master, completes his degeneracy by reducing him from the rank of artisan to that of common workman" (www.geocities.com).

The ways of doing work in traditional times have changed in the present time. The traditional workers, who performed his work with hand tools, have shifted to machines. Utensil-making in traditional times was in the hands of the Thathiars. Some of the Thathiars were also dealing with utensils as agents, contractors and shopkeepers. The whole process of work was manual. The Thathiars involved in utensil making were mainly dependent upon government for raw material. However, they would also procure scrap from local dealers/shopkeepers. These traditional Thathiars made the products and sold it to shopkeepers, contractors, and sometimes directly to the customers. A few contractors played the role of mediator between traditional Thathiars and shopkeepers who purchased finished products from them and sold it to shopkeepers. The shopkeepers sometimes purchased utensils directly from the traditional Thathiars and sometimes from contractors to sell it.

With the diversification of the Thathiars work, the job is now performed by different categories of people, that is, manufacturers, wholesalers, retailers, contractors and skilled workers besides the traditional Thathiars. These days utensil making is performed by traditional Thathiars in their traditional set up and manufactures and skilled workers are engaged in workshops and small-scale factories. In this process, traditional Thathiar is the backbone of the utensil making. In the present time, they purchase raw material from local market. Their process of work has changed. They are using their traditional tools, along with the use of modern machines like electric furnace, fans, electric hammer, shapers etc. Manufacturers have their own independent processing units i.e., small-scale workshops and factories. Their present investment in this work has risen up to lakhs of rupees. Besides the supervision of whole production process, they also participate in the production process. Purchasing of raw material, maintaining quality of the products and supervision of workers are under their control. The range of the workers employed in the factories varies from two to twenty. The study reveals that they are skilled workers (who have skills and experience in the work), daily wage worker, helpers (who are not fully experienced in the factory work). The minimum prevailing wages for workers are Rs 70 to Rs 300 per week which is decided according to the weight of the products produced by them. They are paid Rs 17 per kilogram. Those who are working on permanent basis are paid on monthly basis. Their monthly wages are between Rs 2000 to Rs 3000. The supervision of workers is one of the major problems in setting up of work. Every traditional Thathiar is fully experienced in his work, especially in a single kind of utensil he excels. For instance, some specialise in making *katories* (bowls), while others in making *karahis* (flat surfaced cooking pot). That's why he does not easily get ready to work with manufacturer. With the mechanisation of traditional work, many people got displaced from work, who later became skilled workers in the factories.

Diversification in work also gave rise to some new combinations of work. The selling of the utensils is mainly in the hands of wholesalers and retail shopkeepers. Wholesalers purchase the ready material from the traditional Thathiars, contractors and mainly from manufacturers in a large quantity. They sell largely to the retailers and sometimes to the customers directly. To provide various varieties of products, they sometimes purchase the items from outside the town or state.

Retailers purchase mainly from wholesalers and sometimes from the contractors. The contractors purchase raw material from the market and then give it to the traditional Thathiars and manufacturers to make utensils on contract. Contract period depends on the quantity of material. Contractor fixes the wages according to the days, i.e., Rs 80 per day. After manufacturing process, contractor negotiates with shopkeepers and wholesalers to sell the product with two per cent commission of the total. Some contractors themselves sell the products directly to the customers, while some contractors are engaged in the combined activity of contractor as well as manufacturing.

With the passage of time, technology of work has changed as in the case of the Thathiars of Jandiala Guru. They in the earlier times used tools like hammers of wood and iron. Makhu (a container made of carbon soil in big or small size), Maganu (pattern/mould), Chaka (a round plate or structure of metal), Mekha (nails of small size), a hand blower and Chisel to make variety of utensils. With the use of these tools, they applied techniques of hammering, melting, grinding and shaping. In present times, with the development and advancement of tools, now in place of Maganu they are using readymade pattern for every shape of product. In place of hand blower they use electric furnace, electric machine for polishing and rolling machines are used to make the metals fine and smooth. In the modern times the melting of various metals is done with the help of modern machines. The shapers are available in different patterns. Now rolling machines are used for grinding the metals. Data in this study show that large proportions of respondents are engaged in making different kinds of utensils for cooking and eating. They are traditional Thathiars, manufacturers, manufacturers-cum-contractors and skilled workers. This study reveals that less than fifty per cent of the total Thathiars have introduced changes to diversify and modify the work processes, while the rest of the respondents have not introduced changes because of financial constraints.

No doubt, the technological revolution and the globalisation of market have brought about drastic and rapid changes in the relative importance of individual sectors and occupations in the economy. This means that more and more people will have to adopt a change of job or career involving different skills–during the working life. According to an estimate, 80 per cent of today's skills will become obsolete in 10 years, while over that time 80 per cent of the labour force will possess outdated skills without lifelong learning (www.geocities.com).

Occupations in societies with relatively lower levels of technological differentiation tend to be characterised by stable relationships, both at work and in the community. In highly differentiated occupational societies, these stabilities are so extensive that they render many occupations obsolete and occupational retraining necessary. Social mobility is also accelerated with the change in the income, prestige and social power of occupations. The occupational mobility amongst the Thathiars shows various directions of change in occupation. Intergenerational occupational mobility has been analysed across generations of grandfather, father and son. The study reveals that there was fall in fathers' generation carrying on the activities of traditional Thathiars. This shows father's generation has moved to other occupations as compared to his grandfather's generation. These changes were the result of transformation and development. Advancement in the work process leads to other kinds of work like manufacturing, contractual, trading and skilled work etc. Comparison of father and son's generations indicate that younger generation has no interest to carry on traditional Thathiars work. Difference of this proportion shows that a large number of persons in the present generation have moved towards other jobs/ occupations related to utensil making. The rate of mobility in all these occupations is higher in son's generation which shows horizontal mobility in the occupational structure.

To know about intragenerational occupational mobility, the very first occupation and the present occupation of the respondents have been taken into consideration. It has been found that small proportion of respondents present occupation is traditional Thathiar. In other occupations too, there are changes. Those whose first occupation was manufacturing, with the passage of time, they became contractors along with the manufacturing, while, some became wholesalers from retailers. This shows horizontal mobility in the occupational structure of the Thathiars. These changes are the result of modernisation, transformation and awareness among workers. Every person wants to earn more for better life which motivates them to join work of better choice. It has been found that small proportion of respondents remained stagnant to the traditional Thathiar work. On the other side, a large proportion of respondents changed the first occupation and joined the other occupation in utensil making.

The proportion of traditional Thathiar work has fallen. This shows a pattern of diversification in this work. There is an increase in the proportion of manufacturers, contractors, retail shops of utensils and in skilled workers. Majority of them have joined as skilled workers. Because industrialisation changed the work processes, this gave rise to the modifications, diversification of the occupation. Most of the traditional Thathiars think that it's better to work in others' workshops rather than working independently. Because the raw material is expensive, they are not in position to afford modern technology or machinery. That's why they have joined as skilled workers.

Besides this, very small proportion respondents are those whose first occupation was retail business of clothes, karyana or general items. But the popularity and increase in the demand of metal products influenced them to join this occupation. Some are those whose fathers were in this occupation but they did not join or take it as first occupation. Later they joined the hereditary occupation. With the passage of time, due to advancement in techniques of work, the nature of traditional work has undergone change. A large proportion of children are not interested in pursuing this work. The reasons for not taking up this work are lack of demand, physically tough nature of work and lower status.

It is relevant to mention that levels of transformation make society traditional or modern. The processes of change among Thathiars show that due to industrialisation and resultant transformation, many other kinds of materials like steel, glass, plastic, corning and porcelains etc. have been invented which are used to make utensils of different kinds. Besides this, the use of non-stick utensils, microwave ovens, pressure cookers and other modern appliances for cooking are quite common in modern kitchens. This advancement led to reduction in the demand of metal utensils. As the pattern of industrialisation is not same for all countries, the nature of transformation experienced by different countries is also uneven. The change which has occurred in England and Japan due to the industrial development is different from the transformations which have taken place in India. James' study (2000) depicts that the nineteenth century also brought a crystallisation of the processes that separated the artisanary into productive and retail segments. Historians have traced this process to the eighteenth century in some trades but to the nineteenth in many more, and this, no doubt, is central to the story of the transformation of the artisans.

Besides these studies Thathiars or coppersmith appears in the novel The Big Heart (1945) that leaves many social issues and presents the basic conflict between the forces of tradition and modernity through various forces like the temple and clock and of course through characters.

The theme of the novel is the conflict between hereditary copper smiths and the capitalists. Ananta, the son of a coppersmith, comes from Bombay to his ancestral city; Amritsar where he takes up his traditional profession. But he finds that it is very difficult for him to make both ends meet on account of the introduction of machine. Lala Murli Dhar and Seth Gokul Chand have established a factory. The traditional artisans are unable to stand in competition with factory owner as their hand-made products are in some ways inferior to, and more costly than factory products. Consequently, the demand for them miserably falls down in the market. The rate of piece-work for making utensils has been lowered down. Moreover they are exploited by factory-owners in various ways. Most of the coppersmiths are compelled to close their shops. They are rendered jobless and poor. The factory owners refuse to absorb the jobless artisans (coppersmith) in this factory. Virtually they turn against the factory and its owners, and thus there is a conflict between the two sections of people-the factory owners and the traditional artisans. Ralia, close friend of Ananta, is the most sufferers as it becomes very difficult for him to support his family. The factory owners are not ready to employ him at any cost. So he is also dead against the factory. The introduction of machine has thrown the artisans out of work. But Ananta can realise its usefulness. Unexpected events take place when Ralia, one of the unemployed workers, starts wrecking the machine. The aggression towards machine is so powerful that when Ananta tries to stop this wanton destruction, he got killed when the raging Ralia strike his head against the machine.

To sum up, we can say that with the advent of industrialisation, the artisanal work has changed. The study reveals that a large proportion of Thathiars are moving towards other occupations. They have become small and medium level shopkeepers selling factory made utensils. Those who are educated have become accountants, teachers and advocates etc. Because of the nature of the work and the lower status attached to it, the younger generation shows no interest in this work. Due to the change in their occupation, they now consider themselves as belonging to trading caste. With the change and diversification of their work, they have claimed to move up in the social hierarchy. With the change in the orientation towards work, the Thathiars have emulated a dominant trading caste group, the Khatris. The Khatris are successful in trade and are known for their business acumen. The changes in the traditional artisanal work have made them to identify themselves with Khatris. Thus, Thathiars claim to have Khatri status. The present study reveals that how this backward caste/OBC has attained the higher status in the Varna hierarchy due to changes in their traditional work.

In the end there is a need to theoretically contextualise the transformation which has taken place in the artisan caste of utensil makers that is the Thathiars. The social and economic transformation has occurred in utensil making as a result of industrialisation and the arrival of utensils made up of other metals than the ones used traditionally. The separation between the Thathiars and utensil making has opened tremendous opportunities, both positive and negative for the Thathiars. The better off among them have taken up business whereas the poor Thathiars have joined the working class. An almost economically homogenous caste of the Thathiars has experienced class formation within the caste community. There is reasonable basis to suggest that the better off Thathiars claim the upper caste status by virtue of the change in the occupation. This indication of sanskritisation shows that there has been a strong correspondence between caste and occupation in the case of certain artisan castes such as Lohar, Tarkhan, and Chamar etc. The breakdown in this correspondence is creating conditions for the social transformation for the caste. At the same time, however, the economic heterogeneity within the caste is asserting or contributing negatively to these claims. The case of Thathiars highlights the complex structure of Punjabi society and dynamism that has been generated due to economic transformation in this state.

It may be pointed out that the improvement in the status also involves whether the upper castes accept or endorse these claims of change in status. To what extent, Thathiars are recognised as a caste of higher status is serious problematic if we keep in mind the hereditary character of caste system. One of the major indicators that Thathiars continues to be a caste without Khatri status is the practice of caste endogamy. Thus, the case of Thathiars is no different from the case of other such castes that have experienced change due to industrialisation.

References

Ahuja, Ram. 1993. *Indian Social System*. New Delhi: Rawat Publications.

Anand, Mulk Raj.1945. *The Big Heart*. New Delhi: Arnold-Heinemann Publishers.

Anderson, Nels. 1964. *Dimensions of Work: The Sociology of a Work Culture*. New York: David McKay.

Baden-Powell, B.H. 1872. *Handbook of the Manufactures and Arts of the Punjab*. Lahore: Punjab Printing Company.

Bal, Gurpreet. 1995. *Development and Change in Punjab: A Study of Blacksmiths*. New Delhi: National Book Organization.

Betteille, Andre. 1971. *Caste, Class and Power: Changing Patterns of Stratification in a Tanjore Village*. Berkely: University of California.

Bhandani, B.L. 1999. *Peaseants, Artisans and Entrepreneurs*. Jaipur: Rawat Publications.

Bhattacharya, J.N. 1975. *Hindu Castes and Sects*. Calcutta: N.P. House.

Blunt, E.A.H. 1969. *The Caste System of Northern India: With Special Reference of the United Provinces of the Agra and Oudh*. Delhi: S. Chand & Co.

Bose, P.K., 1982. “Production organisation and market relations of potters of Gujrat”. *Man in India*, Vol. 62 No .3 (Sept.).

Census of India 1921. *Punjab*, Vol. XV. 1923. Lahore: Lahore Printing Press.

Census of India 1991, Punjab District Census Hand Book, Series 20, part XII-A and B Village and Town Directory. Chandigarh: Chandigarh Administration Press.

Chicherov, A.I.: *Economic 1971. India Development in 16th-18th Centuries Moscow*: Nauka Publishing House, Central Department of Oriental Literature.

Crooke, William. 1974. *The Tribes and Castes of the North-Western India*, Vol. III and IV. New Delhi: Cosmo Publication.

Crooke, William. 1987. *Races of Northern India*. Delhi; Cosmo Publication.

D’Souza, V.S. 1985. *Economic Development Social Structure and Population Growth*. New Delhi: Sage Publication.

Dahiya, Neelima. 1986. *Art and Crafts in Northern India from the Earliest Time to C. 200 B.C.* Delhi: B.R. Publishing Corporation.

Dak, T.M., Grover, R.P., Sharma, M.L. 1987. “Industrialisation, Caste Structure and Rural Artisans,” *Guru Nanak Journal of Sociology*, Vol. 8, No.1.

Davis, Kingsley.1957. Human Society. New York: Macmillan Press.

Dirks, Nicholas. B. 2002. *Castes of Mind: Colonialism and the Making of Modern India*. New Delhi: Pauls Press.

Douglas, Heynes. 2006. “Small Products and the Consolidation of the Informal Economy: Artisan-Capitalists and the Transformation of the Informal Economy, 1940-1960”. A Paper Presented at National Seminar on Condition of

Marginal Groups in Contemporary India, Surat: Centre for Social Studies. 5-7 July.

Dube, S.C. 1977. *Tribal Heritage of India*. New Delhi: Vikas Publishing House Pvt. Ltd.

Gadgil, D.R. 1972. *The Industrial Evolution of India in Recent Times 1860-1939*. Bombay: Oxford University Press.

Gahlot, S.S., Dhar, B. 1989. *Castes and Tribes of Rajasthan*. Jodhpur: Jain Brothers.

Gupta, Dipanker. 1991. *Social Stratification*. Bombay: Oxford University Press.

Hall, Richard. 1975. *Occupation and the Social Structure*. Englewood Cliffs: Prentice Hall.

Hanna, Nelly. 2011. *Artisan Entrepreneurs in Cairo and Early Modern Capitalism (1600-1800)*: Syracuse University Press.

Hirszowicz, Maria. 1981. *Industrial Sociology: An Introduction*. Oxford: Martin Robertson and Company Ltd.

Hnatkovska, V., Lahiri, A., and Paul, S.B. (2013). "Breaking the Caste Barrier: Intergenerational Mobility in India". *Journal of Human Resources*, 48(2), 435-473.

Hughes, J, R.T. 1958. "Foreign Trade and Balanced Growth—The Historical Framework", *American Economic Review*, Vol. 49, No. 2, pp. 330-337.

Hutton, J.H. 1951. *Caste in India: Its Nature and Function*, (IV edition). Bombay: Oxford University Press.

Ibbetson, Denzil. 1961. *A Glossary of the Tribes and Castes of the Punjab and the North-West Frontier Province*, Vol. III. Punjab: Patiala Language Department.

Ibbetson, Denzil. 1974. *Punjab Castes*. Delhi: Neeraj Publication House.

James, R. Farr. 2000. *Artisans in Europe 1300-1914*. United Kingdom: Cambridge University Press.

Johal, Daljinder Singh. 1980. "Literary Evidence on Social Structure in the Punjab (1750-1850)," *Journal of Regional History*, Vol. 1.

Johnson, J. Terence. 1972. *Professions and Power*. London: Macmillan Press.

Joshi, K.G.1989. *Migration and Mobility: A Sociological Study of Urban Karnataka*. Delhi: Anand Printing House.

Judge, Paramjit Singh and Bal, Gurpreet. 2006. *Strategies of Social Change in India*. New Delhi M D Publications.

Kashyap, N.N. "Good Progress in Metal Industry", *The Tribune*, Industries Supplement, 3:7, Ambala (28 April, 1957).

Krishnan, Shantha. 1989. *Traditional Potters: Entitlements and Enablements of Artisans*. New Delhi: Indus Publishing Company.

Kumar, Dharma. 1983. *Cambridge Economic History of India*, Vol. II. Cambridge: Cambridge University Press.

Kumar, Nita.1988. The *Artisans of Banaras*: Popular Culture and Identity. New Delhi: Orient Longman.

Kumar, S., Heath, A., and Heath, O. (2002b). Changing Patterns of Social Mobility: Some Trends Over Time. *Economic and Political Weekly*, 37(40), 4091-4096.

Lakshmana, Chintamani. 1973. *Caste Dynamics in Village India*. Bombay: Nachiketa Publications.

Landes, David. S. 2003. *The Unbound Prometheus: Technological Change and Industrial Development in*

Western Europe from 1750 to the Present, (II edition). Cambridge: Cambridge University Press.

Levi-Strauss, Claude. 1977. *Structural Anthropology*, Vol. II. London: Lowe and Brydone Printer.

Lohia, Rammanohar. 1964. *The Caste System*. Hyderabad: India Commercial Printing Press.

Majunder, R. (2010). Intergenerational Mobility in Educational and Occupational Attainment: A Comparative Study of Social Classes in India. Margin: *The Journal of Applied Economic Research*, 4(4), 463-494.

Mandlebaum, David. G. 1972. *Society in India*. Bombay: Popular Parkashan.

McLeod, John. 2004. *The History of India*. London: Greenwood Press.

Mhetras, V.G. 1966. *Labour Participation in Management: an Experiment in Industrial Democracy in India*. Bombay: Manaktalas.

Miller, D.C. and Form, W.H. 1980. *Industrial Sociology: The Sociology of Work Organisations*, (II edition). New York: Harper and Row.

Mishra, R.N. and Rao, D. Tata. 2004. *Rural Artisans in India*. New Delhi: Mohit Publications.

Moore, W.E. 1967. "Industrialisation: Social Aspects", In David L. Sills (ed.), *Encyclopeadia of Social Sciences*, Vol. 7, New York: MacMillan Company and Free Press.

Mukherji, T.N. 1974. *Art Manufacturers of India*. New Delhi: Navrang Publishers.

Pande, Sunanda. 1986. *Trends of Occupational Mobility among Migrants*. Jaipur: Rawat Publications.

Parthasarathy, R. 1999. "Tradition and Change: Artisan Producer in Gujarat," *The Journal of Entrepreneurship*, Vol. 8, No.1.

Pontet, Josette. 1997. "Craftsman and revolution in Bordeaux," in Geoffrey Crossick (ed.) *The Artisans and the European Town, 1500-1900*. Aldershot.

Prasad, Amar Nath. 2001. *Critical Response to Indian Fiction in English*. New Delhi: Atlantic Publishers.

Rai, M. Satya.1986. *Punjab Since Partition*. Delhi: Durga Publications.

Rao, M. Gangadhar. 1992. *Entrepreneurship and Entrepreneurial Development*. Delhi: Kanishka Publications.

Ratra, Kaur, Chhikara. 2006. *Marriage and Family: In Diverse and Changing Scenario*. New Delhi: Deep & Deep Publications.

Reissman, Leonard. 1959. *Class in American Society*. New York: The Free-Press, Collier-Macmillan Ltd.

Roy, Tirthankar.1996. "Home Market and the Artisans in Colonial India: A Study of Brass-Ware", *Modern Asian Studies*, Vol. 30, No. 2, Cambridge University Press.

Russell, R.V. and Hiralal. 1975. *The Tribes and Castes of the Central Provinces of India*, Vol. IV. New Delhi: Cosmo Publication.

Sahay, K.N. 1967. "Caste and Occupation in a Village in Bihar," *Man in India* Vol. 47, No. 3.

Sarkar, J. 1984. *Caste, Occupation and Change*. Delhi: B.R. Publishing Corporation.

Schneider, E.V. 1957. Industrial Sociology: The Social Relations of Industry and the Community. London: McGraw-Hill.

Shah, A.M. 2010. *The Structure of Indian Society: Then and Now*. New Delhi: Routledge Publishers.

Sharma, B.B. 1992. *Encyclopeadia: Dictionary of Sociology*. New Delhi: Anmol Publications.

Sharma, Harish Chander. 1978. "Demographic Distribution of Artisans of the Punjab in the Late Nineteenth Century: Some Problems and Prospects," Proceedings Punjab History Conference. Patiala: Punjabi University.

Sharma, Harish Chander. 1979. "Expression of Caste Mobility Among the Artisans of the Punjab," Proceedings Punjab History Conference. Patiala: Punjabi University.

Sharma, Harish Chander. 1980. "Artisans in the Punjab (1849-1947): Occupational Change and New Social Relations," *Journal of Regional History*, Vol. I. Amritsar.

Sharma, Harish Chander. 1983. "A Note on Urban Artisans of the Punjab," Proceedings of Indian History Conference. Burdwan: Burdwan University.

Sharma, Harish Chander. 1996. *Artisans of the Punjab: A Study of Social Change in Historical Perspective (1849-1947)*. New Delhi: Manohar Publishers.

Sharma, Satish Kumar. 1986. *The Chamar Artisans: Industrialisation, Skills and Social Mobility*. New Delhi: B.R. Publishing Company.

Sharrock, W.W., Hughes, J.A., Martin, P.J., 2003. *Understanding Modern Sociology*. London: Sage Publication Pvt. Ltd.

Sherring, M.A. 1974. *Hindu, Tribes and Castes*. New Delhi: Cosmo Publication.

Shukla, B.R.K. and Anima Shukla, 1981 "Caste and occupation in a North Indian village", *The Eastern Anthropologist*, Vol. 34, No. 1, Jan-March.

Singh, K.S. 1998. *India's Communities*, Vol. VI. Delhi: Oxford University Press.

Singh, R.S. 1986. *Changing Occupational Structure of Scheduled Tribes.* New Delhi: Inter-India Publications.

Sinha, Jai. B.P. 1990. *Work Culture in the Indian Context.* New Delhi: Sage Publications.

Smelser, Neil. J. 1963. *The Sociology of Economic Life.* Englewood Cliffs: Prentice-Hall.

Srinivas, M.N. 1972. *Social Change in Modern India.* Bombay: Orient Longman.

Tandon, Parkash. 1961. *Punjabi Century*. New Delhi: Orient Longman.

Thapar, Romila. 1968. *A History of India*, Vol. I. Harmonds-Worth: Penguin Books.

Tripathy, S.N., Dash, C.R. 1997. *Migrant Labour in India*. New Delhi: Discovery Publishing House.

Vries, De. 1994. "The Industrial Revolution and the Industrious Revolution," *Journal of Economic History,* Vol. 54, No. 2.

Wadhawan, Raj. 1972. "Report on Historical Evolution of Amritsar City," A M. Phil Dissertation Submitted For The Degree of N.C.R.P. to Guru Nanak Dev University, Amritsar.

Weber, Max.1950. *General Economic History*, translated by Frank H.Knight. New York: The Free Press of Glencoe.

WEBSITES:

www.sociologyguide.com

www.culturaleconomics.atfree

Michael Teaching- The Artisan Role.htm

Message from michael.com

Metalkondagaon.PDF-9327F093-eedc-4

en.wikipedia.org/wiki/caste

www.chowk.com

realinfo.tv/index.php?topic=8110.0.

Sahistory.html

www.geocities.com

www.books.google.co.in/books/?isbn=8126905867

www.tribuneindia.com/2005/20015006/a plus.htm#2

INTERVIEW SCHEDULE

The Thathiars: A Sociological Study of Changes in an Artisan Caste in Punjab

Con□dential Serial No.__________

1. PERSONAL INFORMATION

1.1 Name : ______________________________

1.2 Sex (Male/Female) : ______________________________

1.3 Age : ______________________Years

1.4 Marital Status : Married/Unmarried/ Divorced

1.5 Religion : ______________________________

1.6 Caste ______________ Sub-Caste ________________

1.7 Education : ______________________________

1.8 Occupation : ______________________________

1.9 Household Information

Relation with the respondents	*Age*	*Marital status*	*Educa-tion*	*Occup-ation*	*Income (in Rs)*

1.10 Family Type : Joint/Nuclear/ Extended

1.11 Place of Residence__________ Ward No. __________

1.12 Place of Work____________ Ward No. ___________

1.13 Were you born at this place (   ) or have come from other place (   ) or are you a commuter (   ).

1.14 If born at this place, was your father or grandfather also born at this place?

Grandfather : Yes/No

Father : Yes/ No

1.15 (If migrated) when did you migrate : _________Year

From which place : ___________

Village/Town/City : ____________

District : ____________

Why did you migrate to this town?

(a) ____________________________

(b) ____________________________

(c) ____________________________

1.16 (If commuter), place from where you are commuting.

Place : ____________

Village/ Town/ City : ____________

District : ____________

Distance : ____________

Mode of Commuting : Bus/ Scooter/ Cycle

Why do you commute? Give reasons?

(a) ____________________________

(b) ____________________________

(c) ____________________________

2. CHANGES IN THE CASTE SYSTEM

2.1 Can you enlist the different caste groups in your town according to their status?

1. ____________ 2. ____________

3. ____________ 4. ____________

5. ____________ 6. ____________

2.2 Which caste is at the top of hierarchy in your town?

____

2.3 Which caste in your view is at the bottom of hierarchy in your town?

____

2.4 Which is the dominant caste in your town? Why, give reasons?

(a) ____

(b) ____

(c) ____

2.5 Where would you place your own caste in the caste hierarchy?

(a) Top

(b) Middle

(c) Low

2.6 Do you believe in high or low status of caste in the society? Yes/No

If yes, what are the reasons?

____

If No, why?

____

2.7 Do you think people can change their caste position? Yes/No

If Yes, how ______________________________

If No, why ______________________________

Records give us information that Thathiar (your original caste) is an artisan caste (servicing, middle range caste). But, now you have become Khatri (which is high, trading caste).

How did it happen in your caste?

When did it happen (Approximate)?

Have you ever tried to know the reasons for doing so?

Emergence OF ECONOMIC INEQUALITIES WITH IN THE CASTE

3.1 Representation in social and political spheres.

3.1.1 Do you think that the customs/practices of your caste are different

from other castes in any way? Yes/No

If yes, what are the distinctive features?

3.1.2 Do you marry within your own caste? Yes/No

3.1.3 Do you select mate out of all the sub-castes of your caste? Yes/No

If no, which sub caste do you avoid and why?

Is there any case/cases of inter-caste/inter-religion marriages in your caste group in the town?

3.1.5 Do you have social relations with these caste people?

	Social Relations	High	Middle	Low

	Inviting/ attending to birth/ marriage/ death ceremonies			
	Participating in family functions.			
	Casual get together at family level/ interdining.			
	Residential proximity/ neighbourhood relations			

3.1.6 Do you have any caste association? : Yes/No

If yes, then are you member of the association? : Yes/No

If yes, name of the association you are member:

____

Number of members:

____

Type of activities performed:

____

3.1.7 Do you have information about other caste associations in your town? Yes/No

If Yes, Name: ____________________

No. of members: ____________________

Activities: ____________________

3.2 Representation in religious spheres

3.2.1 Do you have any religious place of your caste to worship? Yes/No

If yes, which are the places?

____

3.2.2 To whom you worship?

____

3.2.3 What are your religious beliefs, rituals? Specify.

____

Whether the members of other caste/communities come to attend the religious functions? Yes/No

If yes, which caste group : ________________

Which communities : ________________

3.3 Interpersonal and Intercaste relations

3.3.1 Who in the town are your personal friends with whom you interact regularly?

Name	Caste Background	Occupation

3.3.2 Who in the town are your family friends?

Name	Caste	Occupation

3.3.3 Do you think there are some direct/indirect restrictions upon you by your caste group for inter-relationships with other caste groups? Yes/No

If No, with which caste groups do you have inter-relations?

	Caste groups of the town	Interdining	Intermarriage
1	Khatri		
2	Brahmin		
3	Arora		
4	Jat		
5	Tank-Kshatriya		
6	Other		

3.3.4 What is the usual reaction of other caste groups when invited by you on any occasions of happiness or sorrow?

1. Happily visit : ____________
2. Unwillingly visit : ____________
3. Never visit : ____________
4. Any other : ____________

4. CHANGES IN OCCUPATION

4.1 Skill Formation

4.1.1 What is the nature of your work?

____

4.1.2 When did you start your present work? ______ Year.

4.1.3 What motivated you to take up this occupation?

____

____

4.1.4 How did you learn the skills? Hereditary skill/on -the- job/ format training?

____

4.1.5 What was your age when you learnt the skills?

____

4.1.6 What activities you perform in the whole production process?

____

____

4.1.7 If utensil making and selling is not your hereditary occupation, then, did you face any difficulties in the setting up of the enterprise of working in it? Yes/No

If yes, type of difficulties faced.

____

If no, why?

____

____

4.1.8 How did your hereditary skills help in establishing your enterprise?

____

____

4.2 Techniques of work and work organisation

4.2.1 What type of technology/techniques you use in your work?

____

____

____

4.2.2 What type of things are produced and repaired by you?

	Name of items(s)	Production/Repair
1.	____________	________
2.	____________	________

4.2.3 Do you perform any rituals before starting your work every day?

____

____

4.2.4 What are your working hours?

____

4.2.5 How many holidays you observe in a week?

____

4.2.6 What would be your approximate investment?

Initial investment Rs ______________

Present investment Rs ______________

4.2.7 Do the members of your family also participate in the work with you? Yes/No

If yes, who are the members? What activities they perform?

____

____

____

4.2.8 What is the role of women and children in the work process?

____

____

4.2.9 Who else participate in the working?

(a) Skilled worker

(b) Daily wage worker

(c) Helpers

(d) Any other

4.2.10 (If worker) Do you get daily wages/monthly.

____

4.2.11 What are your wages?

____

4.2.12 Do you get bonus or annual increment from your owner?

If yes, How much? ______________

If no, what are the reasons? ______________

____

4.3 Raw Material and Market

4.3.1 What are your sources of raw material?

____

4.3.2 From where do you get the raw material?

____

4.3.3 (If manufacturer) Do you face any problem while getting raw material? Yes/No

If yes, what type of problems?

(a) With regard to supply

(b) Controlled price

(c) Transportation

(d) Quantity / Requirement

4.3.4 How do you sell your products?

(a) Through open market

(b) Intermediate

(c) Any other

4.3.5 If in the market then

(a) Local market

(b) Within the state

(c) Out of state

(d) Exports

4.3.6 Do you face any marketing problems? : Yes/No

If yes, specify

4.4 Transformations in production process

4.4 .1 Have made any change in your work over the time?

(a) Diversified

(b) Modified

(c) No change

If no change, what were the reasons?

4.4.2 What were the reasons responsible to introduce change in your work and production process?

4.4.3 What are the changes you introduced/experienced in your work?

(a) Mode of work

(b) Place of work

(c) Organisational changes

(d) Joining of other castes

(e) Increase in profits

4.4.4 What type of new machines or techniques you have introduced in your work over the years?

____

____

4.4.5 Do you feel modern machines are better than the traditional tools in terms of:

		Yes/ No	Reasons
1.	Efficiency	________	________
2.	Durability	________	________
3.	Productivity	________	________
4.	Profitability	________	________

4.5 Political Organisation

4.5.1 Are you aware of any organisation consisting of Thathiars? Yes/No

4.5.2 If yes, are you member of any organisation through which you carry on your work activities? Yes/No

If yes, name of the organisation

____

No. of members______________________

Level of participation__________________

Nature of activities performed ____________

4.5.3 Do you have any labour union in the town?

If yes, no. of unions (specify the names)

____

No. ofmembers : ______________________

Types of activities

____

4.5.4 In case of any dispute do you consult any union? Yes/No

If yes, which union (specify the name)

____

Role of union

____

Types of activities performed

____

4.5.5 Are these organisations looking into your interests? Yes/No

If yes, in what way?

____

5. OCCUPATIONAL MOBILITY

5.1 What was the occupation of your father and grandfather?

	First Occupation	Last Occupation
Father	__________	__________
Grandfather	__________	__________

5.2 Have your grandfather and father ever got engaged in utensil making/ selling?

Grandfather Yes/No

Father Yes/No

5.3 Where were they carrying the work?

Father : ____________________

Grandfather : ____________________

5.4 If respondent's job is different than his father, then why did you change your work? Give reasons?

____

____

5.5 What are the changes you have experienced in your work over the time?

	Year of joining	Year of leaving
First occupation	________	________
Second occupation	________	________
Third occupation	________	________

5.6 Are your children interested in this work?

Yes/No Can't Say

If no, what are the reasons?

____

If yes, why?

____

5.7 Is there any one from your family (brother, uncle) who has changed the traditional occupation?

Yes, No

If yes, to which occupation they have changed.

Relation with Respondent	Nature of present occupation	Reasons for changes
________	________	________
________	________	________

Index

L

M

N

O

P

R

S